Gardening with
the New Small Plants

Gardening
with the
New Small Plants

The Complete Guide to
Growing Dwarf and Miniature Shrubs,
Flowers, Trees and Vegetables

Oliver E. Allen

Houghton Mifflin Company · Boston 1987

Library of Congress Cataloging-in-Publication Data
Allen, Oliver E.
Gardening with the new small plants.
Bibliography: p.
Includes index.
1. Gardening.   2. Miniature plants.   3. Dwarf shrubs.
4. Dwarf fruit trees.   5. Midget vegetables.   I. Title.
II. Title: Small plants.   III. Title: Dwarf and minia-
ture shrubs, flowers, trees, and vegetables.
SB454.3.S53A45   1987   635   86-21492
ISBN 0-395-39395-7

Printed in the United States of America

R 10 9 8 7 6 5 4 3 2 1

Line drawings by Mary Rankin

FRONTISPIECE: Dwarf and miniature plants, including
two specially sheared dwarf Alberta spruces (*Picea
glauca* 'Conica'), grace a New England rock garden
designed by Bill Brady and Gary Mottau.
(Photo by Gary Mottau)

Acknowledgments

Any subject as wide-ranging as small plants necessitates dipping into a multitude of specialized fields, each virtually a world unto itself. Few plantspeople are expert in more than a few of these, and the author (whose background is journalism) qualifies in none. I have thus been totally dependent on those who have made it their business — and/or their pleasure — to know all about one or more of the categories, and to all I extend my gratitude.

Leading the list is Jim Cross of Cutchogue, New York, nurseryman extraordinary, wise counselor and valued friend. Jim suggested approaches, recommended other consultants, answered questions cheerfully and constructively, provided pertinent criticism at every stage and read much of the copy — exhibiting an eagle eye for detail that was both astonishing and invaluable. The book could not have been the same without him.

A handful of good souls were particularly helpful in explaining abstruse subject matter and devoting time to show this neophyte the marvels of their specialty: Warren Berg, Tom Dilatush, Priscilla Galpin, Harold Greer, Polly Hill, Jean Iseli, Mareen Kruckeberg, Dorothy Metheny, John Oliver and Hank Schannen.

For reading parts of the text or for other assistance I am also grateful to Bob Badger, Ellie Brinckerhoff, Dick Bush, Frank Cabot, Tom Cooper, Connie Cross, Bob Fincham, William Hamilton, Professor Tony Hopfinger, Richard Jaynes, W. Bradford Johnson, Joann Knapp, Fred McGourty, John Mitsch, Rudy Nabel, Eddie Rezek, Harm Saville, John Saville, George Schenk, Professor Sidney Waxman, Ed Wood, and Elizabeth Woodburn.

Special thanks go to Lothian Lynas of the New York Botanical Garden Library, who was unfailingly helpful on sources.

The idea for the book came originally from my editor, Frances Tenen-baum, whose enthusiasm and good sense have helped speed the whole project, and I am much in her debt.

And, as always, I salute Deborah Allen, who knew about plants and liked them long before I ever noticed them at all.

O.E.A.

Contents

Gardening with
the New Small Plants

1

The Wide World of Small Plants

THERE IS SOMETHING ALMOST MAGICAL about a garden of dwarfs, miniatures and other small-scale plants. Here are healthy, robust trees, shrubs and other plants, most of them hardy to subfreezing temperatures, all handsomely proportioned and many producing copious bloom in season. But they are all a fraction of the size of their normal counterparts — creatures seemingly out of a midget fairyland. Viewing them, one has the sense of looking through the wrong end of a telescope, or of being somehow far away, suspended in a balloon high above them.

Yet close inspection shows this small world to be wonderfully real: spruces and pines eighteen inches tall instead of ten feet, elegant rhododendrons and azaleas a foot high instead of four or five, lustily blossoming rose bushes a mere eight inches tall, yellow trumpet daffodils that barely reach four or five inches, geraniums that will never exceed six inches — the range is astonishing. And these plants have not been artificially miniaturized by drastic pruning, for they are not bonsai, deliberately starved and snipped to stay small. They just happen, for one reason or another, to be extremely minute.

The domain of small-scale plants for outdoor gardens is one that increasingly absorbs and excites large numbers of people. For many gardeners they are heaven-sent, the perfect solution. As land values skyrocket, more and

OPPOSITE: The bewitching but almost unreal look of a garden of small plants is delightfully demonstrated in the Branklyn Garden in Perth, Scotland. (Photo by Gary Mottau)

more gardeners find themselves living in condominiums and other kinds of smaller dwellings that present reduced space in which to raise plants. City dwellers look for better ways to set out gardens on balconies, rooftops and terraces — where miniature and dwarf shrubs, trees or flowers can be especially appropriate and attractive.

But it is not just those who are cramped for gardening space who discover smaller plants are well suited to their needs. The burgeoning ranks of older citizens welcome the chance to keep a garden that is pleasing but easier to maintain. Homeowners looking for shrubbery to enhance their yards find that compact or dwarf trees and bushes have the great advantage of growing slowly: a well-designed plan will not become obsolete in a few years. Dedicated plantspeople, who have long since established elaborate perennial beds and cutting gardens that seem to occupy every square foot of available planting space, find they can wedge in a new array of diminutive plants to provide an entirely different horticultural look and simultaneously expand their gardening horizons. Meanwhile a great many gardeners of every level of expertise are discovering that small-scale plants are fun to grow for their own sake. Anyone entering the field learns that it is a rich one — and getting richer all the time.

Both Japanese and English gardeners, confronted as they are with limited space for growing, have long been aware of the joys and advantages of small plants. In the United States, but for different reasons, rock gardeners have been at the center of the movement, seeking out as they constantly do the rare or hitherto unknown alpine plants (many extraordinarily small) that look so good in their carefully managed rockeries. But the field is wider than the recondite alpine-growing world would suggest. For in addition to the dwarf evergreen trees and shrubs, the heathers and miniature bulbs that grace the usual rock gardens, the field can properly be said to include such disparate items as dwarf fruit trees, miniature roses, small-scale annuals like dwarf marigolds and even miniature vegetables. One can have a three-by-five-foot kitchen garden furnishing peas and corn in quantity, or even a midget perennial border.

The kinds of small plants available to the gardener are, furthermore, increasing all the time as botanizers locate new species in the wild and as creative nurserymen and horticultural researchers come upon or develop novel strains in their fields and greenhouses. Time was when the odd undersized plant cropping up in a nursery or greenhouse would invariably be rogued out as unsuitable as well as unsellable. No more. The small are now valued for their own sake — and find a ready market.

What do we mean when we say a plant is small-scale? What makes a miniature, or a dwarf? In truth, there is no fixed standard, for all such terms are relative. Most miniature roses, for example, are larger than crocuses —

which in their natural state just happen to be tiny. Similarly, a "dwarf" hemlock may be fifteen feet high; it just happens to be much smaller than a conventional hemlock. The lack of any universal standard of measurement vexes many thoughtful nurserymen, who plead in vain for some kind of agreement on what "small" or "miniature" really connotes; meanwhile the consumer must patiently adjust to varying figures. This book deals with plants that are miniature or scaled-down versions of other species, sometimes half or a quarter as big, sometimes only a small fraction the size. Two categories of plants are nevertheless discussed here that are not smaller versions of others: heaths and heathers, and alpines. They are included because, depending on the temperature zone, they are likely to be important ingredients of any small-scale garden.

Another key question is: how big will the plant become? Miniature herbaceous plants like dwarf iris or miniature tulips never get a chance to increase in size, of course, as they die back at the end of the season. But dwarf woody plants grow much the same way as their larger counterparts do — just far more slowly. It is simply a question of time. Whereas a conventional spruce tree will shoot up to ten or fifteen feet in a few years, the dwarf spruce that is nine inches high today will probably take many years even to reach eighteen inches — and its growth thereafter may be so slow as to be virtually unnoticeable. As a nurseryman remarked to one customer

The term "dwarf" is a relative one, merely indicating that the plant is smaller than the norm. Thus a dwarf fruit tree, five to seven feet tall, is almost as large as a full-sized rhododendron. Some dwarfing, furthermore, is much more radical than others: while a dwarf rhododendron may be just half the size of a conventional one, a dwarf conifer may be only a tenth as large as its full-sized cousin.

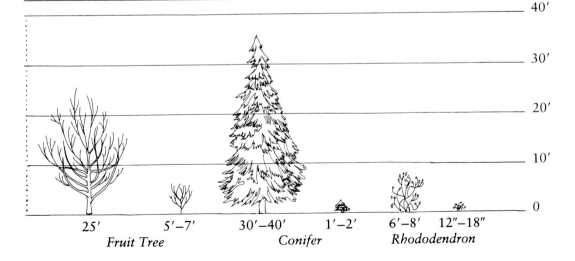

				40'
				30'
				20'
				10'
				0

25'   5'–7'   30'–40'   1'–2'   6'–8'   12"–18"
Fruit Tree   *Conifer*   *Rhododendron*

who asked how long it might take for his new dwarf weeping hemlock to attain a certain dimension, "How patient are you?" To put it another way, that dwarf hemlock may someday grow to a "normal" height — but no one alive today will be around to see it.

Plants can be small either by being controlled or manipulated by humans or by occurring that way in nature. Manipulation can take many forms — none of which produces a true miniature or dwarf. Incessant pruning will keep any plant in bounds, as weary hedge clippers well know, and a particularly artful kind of pruning, when combined with other controls, results in bonsai (a specialized technique not treated in this book). Starving a plant will keep it small, if indeed it survives at all; bonsai's root pruning helps accomplish this, and the tiny trees that grow from quaking bogs stay small because, while they get ample water, the nutrition available to them is scant. Keeping a plant in a constricting container will slow its growth by cramping its roots, and frequent transplanting will also impede it by upsetting its normal processes. Skilled hybridizers can often breed dwarfs by crossing certain likely species; this has produced a number of dwarf rhododendron varieties and even some miniature bulbs. And occasionally dwarfs can be obtained by inducing genetic mutations through the use of radiation, or by feeding a plant synthetic growth inhibitors.

Dwarfing or miniaturizing can occur in nature — that is, without human intervention — in either of two ways. The first is environmental: plants can develop a smaller form in response to the rigors of cold or other demands. Thus alpine plants are those that have become capable of surviving the low temperatures, harsh winds, copious rainfall and swift runoff of mountain slopes; they are low enough to escape the worst effects of the wind, and their roots often reach deep into the ground to pick up any available moisture. Luckily, many alpines can be grown away from their natural habitat if given proper soil, plenty of moisture and flawless drainage. Heaths and heathers have acquired their low stature so as to exist on bleak open moors that seldom warm up. Most dwarf rhododendrons derive from cold, rarefied mountainous areas in southern or eastern Asia. Such plants usually retain their low, compact form after being brought to other environments, but some will become larger when given more warmth or a longer day length, necessitating minor pruning to keep them from achieving unacceptable size.

The other main cause of dwarfing is genetic mutation: something can occur within a plant's cells to cause it to grow differently from others of its type, with the result that it may become prostrate or pendulous, exhibit other unlikely characteristics, or merely grow incredibly slowly. Plants revealing such mutations can show up in the wild or in any large nursery planting, where they are sometimes called "sports." Most plants of this type that are sold today derive from ones that mutated in nurseries, where they

Dwarf perennials and alpines highlight a woodside rock garden ringed by
small-scale conifers. (Photo by Pamela Harper)

were spotted growing among normal plants, set aside for special handling
and subsequently propagated; in the wild such dwarfs are unlikely to survive
for long, as their normal brethren soon grow high enough to cut off their
light. (One exception: as hemlocks can tolerate shade, many dwarf hemlocks survive in the forest.) A feature of most mutated plants is that although
they can be propagated by cuttings, whose products will probably exhibit
identical dwarf characteristics, any seed they produce is likely to result in a
plant that performs normally. Yet some mutated plants found in the wild,
like weeping hemlocks, tend to yield true dwarfs from seed.

   An important thing to note is that mutations can occur in just about any
species. Some species are more prone to mutate than others, but in general
it can be said that the possibilities of miniaturization are well-nigh limitless:
almost any plant can yield a dwarf.

A special train of events results in dwarf fruit trees. In their case, the dwarfing is the result of a minor genetic mutation, but grafting is invoked to make the trees perform satisfactorily. In some cases a dwarf tree is bud-grafted onto a normal rootstock, but more frequently it is the rootstock that has the dwarfing trait, acting as a brake on the otherwise conventional growth of the tree that shows above ground. The resulting fruit may actually be even better than what would grow on an ungrafted dwarf, but the tree maintains its low silhouette, providing for easy maintenance and picking.

Another oddity is that some mutations can show up on an otherwise totally normal tree or shrub: in one spot a kind of extraneous abnormal growth will appear, often rather bristly because its internodes — the spaces between growing points — are so close together. Cuttings made from such "witch's brooms" generally yield dwarf plants, and they are a rich source of dwarf conifers as well as other trees and plants. But the rest of the tree will grow tall.

Just how mutations occur is not completely understood. What is known is that normal plant growth is to a considerable extent dependent on the plant's ability to manufacture hormones, of which the most important are those known as auxins and gibberellins. It is the auxins that enable cells to elongate and divide, a prerequisite to all growth. But scientists have learned that gibberellins must also be present if such growth is not to be retarded. Experts believe that it is a plant's inadequate stream of these substances that brings about dwarfing, although how the hormones actually work is a mystery. When gibberellins are injected into a dwarf plant it will begin to grow normally; but take a cutting from the injected plant — which may now appear normal — and it will yield a dwarf.

Perhaps the most remarkable thing about such "genetic cripples," as one expert has called them, is that they can be so beautiful. While some are admittedly a bit grotesque, most are highly decorative in the garden. Who would think that a plant's genetically caused inability to hold its branches inclined upward or even stretched directly out would result in the handsome "weepers" that are so highly prized? Or that the short internodes could produce an extremely dense, bushy look that goes so well with other plants — but is so different from the appearance of the unmutated plant?

Most dwarf plants, despite their being technically crippled, are healthy and exhibit no weaknesses aside from their odd growth pattern. But their foliage can be unusually striking. Mutation can keep the foliage in its juvenile state, creating leaves or needles that are smaller than — or different in other ways from — those the plant would bear in its adulthood. More remarkably, the foliage can be yellow for part or all of the year, or bluish — or it can be variegated, some of it yellow but the rest green. Some dwarf conifers begin each year with yellow foliage but finish it with green; the length of time spent with yellow leaves actually promotes dwarfing, as yellow inhibits the process of photosynthesis which is so vital to growth.

The chief drawback to mutated plants is their potential instability. What mutates away from normal, it turns out, can mutate back again on occasion, a phenomenon known as reversion mutation. Reversion mutation can suddenly send a slow-growing one-foot-high plant shooting upward in normal growth, and it can alter the mutated foliage on another. A horizontal grower can start sending up vertical shoots way out at the ends of its branches, much to the owner's consternation. Certain species seem more prone to this kind of odd behavior than others: the most popular dwarf holly, *Ilex crenata*, is noted for its instability, as are most dwarf cultivars of the Norway spruce, *Picea abies*. Enthusiasts of small-scale plants are likely to take such aberrations in their stride, feeling that the unexpected is a fair part of the game. Reversion mutations, as a matter of fact, are fairly rare.

One drawback to small-scale plants as a group, in the eyes of some gardeners, is the difficulty that may manifest itself in combining them with others, as they present an entirely different scale. There is no denying the problem — nor are there any easy solutions. Indeed, in any matters of taste it is risky to set rules. And surely there are many instances where a lone dwarf conifer or compact azalea will fit in agreeably with an existing planting. In general, however, it is probably a good idea to set the small plants off by themselves, away from conventional trees and plants that might detract from them or make them seem puny. This is, of course, exactly what rock gardeners do: they create a simulation of an alpine scene that can be viewed as a distinct entity away from other distractions. If you find it necessary to place the smaller species not far from larger plants, you may want to locate them in front of some neutral object or planting, like a hedge or wall, to minimize the conflict. There are, of course, some larger species that make good companion plants to dwarfs and miniatures, and these will be noted during the course of this volume. For some general thoughts on designing, see chapter 12.

But if there are challenges in using small-scale plants in the garden, there are also great rewards. For the distinctive shapes of many of them make their use especially intriguing. A conventional spruce, for example, is always going to be conical; but a dwarf spruce can be globular, pendulous or ground-hugging, as well as conical in a number of different ways. The possibilities of creating striking effects with form and color are virtually endless.

Choosing small-scale plants for the garden can sometimes be a bit confusing, for the nomenclature of some of the plants and trees has become fearfully complicated. Because dwarfing can take many forms and because mutation is unpredictable, many varieties and cultivars have been named

The extraordinary variety that can be achieved in a small backyard by the use of dwarf plants is demonstrated by the Malverne, New York, garden of Ed Rezek, a highly expert amateur collector and grower of small conifers. (Photo by Edward F. Rezek)

only to be proven identical to something previously under cultivation. Progressive nurserymen are doing their best to simplify things and arrive at a universally acceptable system, but in the meantime some labels can be mystifying.

One way to proceed is to consider the numerous varieties and cultivars of each species that are listed at the end of each of the following chapters, and make a preliminary judgment as to what you might like to grow. Then visit a good local garden center or, more appropriately, a specialty nursery that deals with the plants you have in mind. (Specialty nurseries can be recommended by plant societies, botanical gardens or arboretums, but a good number are listed in the Appendix.) In many cases, a skilled nurseryman can best recommend the particular variety or cultivar that will do well in your area and under your growing conditions. Examine what he has to offer and pick out a plant that pleases you. The chances are you will find something absolutely entrancing, and you will be on your way to becoming a devoted small-scale gardener.

Some Botanical Terms

Species: The basic classification unit of botany (and of the other natural sciences). A species comprises individual plants that are so nearly alike in their more stable characteristics that they might have descended from the same parent.

Genus: The next higher category above species, comprising groups of species that have certain structural characteristics in common. The binomial system of designating plants and other living things is based on the genus and the species names combined. Thus *Picea* is the name for the spruce genus; *Picea pungens* is the Colorado spruce, a species. Botanical custom decrees that the genus name be capitalized, the species not; both are italicized.

Family: A group of plants comprising a few — or many — genera that share certain traits. Thus the *Picea* genus is a member of the pine family, the Pinaceae, which also includes the firs *(Abies)*, the cedars *(Cedrus)*, the larches *(Larix)* and the hemlocks *(Tsuga)* in addition to the pines and a few others. (The chamaecyparises, junipers and arborvitaes, however, are in the cypress family, the Cupressaceae.)

Variety: A subdivision of a species, describing plants that form a fairly distinct grouping that has come about through the action of nature (as opposed to human manipulation), but not so distinct as to warrant designation as a separate species. It is usually designated by a third Latin name added to the genus and species, as in *Picea pungens glauca,* the Colorado spruce variety whose foliage is especially blue. Varieties, like species, generally come true from seed though there are occasional aberrations.

Hybrid: A plant that has been brought about via human manipulation — by cross-breeding species or varieties.

Cultivar: Short for "cultivated variety": a variety that has come about through human action, for example through hybridizing. Cultivars are always listed with single quotes around the name, which is capitalized: thus *Picea pungens* 'Koster' is Koster's blue spruce. Cultivars rarely come true from seed and must be propagated asexually (vegetatively), by cuttings or grafting.

Cultivariant: This term is sometimes used to denote a special kind of cultivar that has a different look because it was propagated from wood other than that usually used. Conifers, for example, are most frequently propagated from cuttings taken near the top of the plant; but if the cutting is made from one of the tree's lower branches — which lack the tendency to grow erect — the result (at least initially) will be a horizontally growing plant instead of one with upright form. Many dwarf conifers sold as true recumbent or prostrate plants are actually cultivariants.

2

Dwarf Conifers

PERHAPS THE BIGGEST SURPRISE awaiting anyone who sees a collection of dwarf conifers for the first time is the extraordinary variety of the shapes they have assumed. The look of normal conifers tends to be fairly uniform: firs, hemlocks or spruces rise up in stately grandeur, tapering gracefully to a narrow or pointed top fifty or seventy-five feet in the air; in a grove they can look almost alike to the casual observer. But the forces that bring about dwarfing work their wiles in strange ways. Some dwarf trees do look a bit like their full-size cousins except for being much smaller and bushier. Others "weep," their branches growing outward and then hanging straight down. Many will be globular — perfect round balls that look for all the world like creatures of topiary. A few may be "fastigiate," their branches reaching almost vertically upward so that the entire plant is a small but extremely narrow column. One or two may be "plumose," their limbs spraying out at an angle like plumes on a cap. A large number will be horizontal growers, forming low shrublike masses or even lying prostrate on the ground as if poured from a pitcher. And here and there will be a plant so contorted as virtually to defy description.

For all their weird configurations, almost all have undeniable charm, and many are absolutely beautiful. But dwarf conifers are to be recommended for other reasons as well. They are easy to maintain, for the most part reliably hardy, and generally untroubled by diseases and other such problems. Most are evergreen (larches are a notable exception) and thus ornament the garden year round. For most people who garden on a small scale the conifers will be the "bare bones" of their entire scheme, the basic plants

A Hinoki cypress, *Chamaecyparis obtusa* 'Kosteri', exhibits variegated foliage. Some conifer foliage changes color in midseason, or it may vary depending on the garden's temperature zone. (Photo by Harold E. Greer)

OPPOSITE: A display of dwarf conifers at Jim Cross's wholesale nursery on Long Island indicates the wide range of textures and colors offered by these plants. At left rear is the yellowish *Chamaecyparis pisifera* 'Filifera Aurea Nana'; next to it is a bluish *Picea pungens* 'Glauca Compacta' and a *Chamaecyparis obtusa* 'Pygmaea'. The next row down contains a darker green, rounded *Chamaecyparis pisifera* and a threadleaf Japanese maple, *Acer palmatum* 'Dissectum'. The whitish conifer at center left is a *Chamaecyparis pisifera* 'Mikko', and below it is a *Pinus densiflora*. Trailing over the ground at bottom is a *Juniperus procumbens* 'Nana'. (Photo by Michael Carlebach)

around which the overall garden layout will be designed. The plants oblige by growing so slowly — gaining an inch a year is fast for some of them — that relocating is kept to a minimum. No one planning a small garden would want to be without a few.

The dilemma would come in trying to limit the choice to just a few, so rich is the offering. Half a century ago there were some two hundred fifty varieties and cultivars known to horticulturists. Today the figure is well over fifteen hundred and climbing. Not only do botanical explorers keep coming upon new strains, but creative nurserymen and amateur enthusiasts have found ways to induce innumerable variations and new looks. One imaginative grower, the late Oregon conifer specialist Jean Iseli, claimed that every single species is capable of producing all the different dwarfed forms or shapes in the book. "You've never seen a dwarf weeping Colorado spruce or a fastigiate balsam fir? I'll find it for you. Because I know it must exist somewhere."

Before one even gets to the large number of species, the list of genera — the basic tree groups — is surprisingly long, and every full-size conifer has its multiple dwarf varieties. There are the firs (the genus *Abies*), the arborvitaes *(Thuja)*, the cedars *(Cedrus)*, the true cypresses *(Cupressus)*, the false cypresses *(Chamaecyparis)*, the cryptomerias, the junipers *(Juniperus)*, the spruces *(Picea)*, the pines *(Pinus)*, the yews *(Taxus)* and the hemlocks *(Tsuga)*.

These eleven are basic; but there are others to tempt the devotee, in particular the two West Coast conifer groups, the redwoods *(Sequoia)* and the giant sequoias *(Sequoiadendron)*, both of which — believe it or not — have their dwarf versions, and the two major deciduous conifers, the larches *(Larix)* and the dawn redwoods *(Metasequoia)*. It is a formidable array that nature has provided, and telling them apart (see the list that follows page 17) can sometimes be tricky, for the spruces, firs and hemlocks bear striking resemblances to each other and it can sometimes take an educated and practiced eye to discern certain junipers or arborvitaes from certain false cypresses. To compound the confusion, familiar names can be misleading: the tree known as a red cedar is really a juniper, and the tree often called white cedar is actually *Chamaecyparis thyoides*.

The occasional difficulty in telling one from another should not, however, get in the way of simply enjoying them, or of becoming intrigued by the mysterious ways in which some of them have come to be the way they are. A few dwarf conifers have acquired their reduced stature in response to environmental stresses, the most notable being the dwarf balsam fir (*Abies balsamea* 'Nana'), which is familiar to treeline hikers in the White Mountains of New England, and the dwarf mountain pine or *Pinus mugo* of Europe. Only by acquiring a low profile could such plants survive the icy

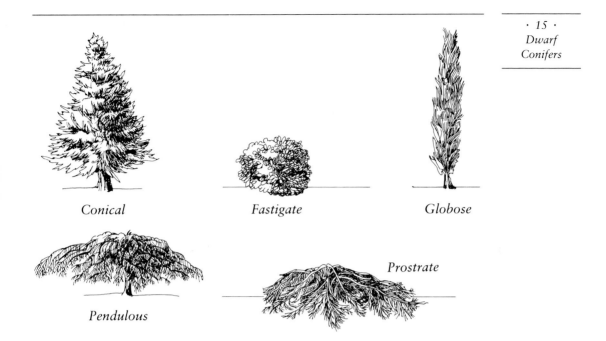

Conical

Fastigate

Globose

Pendulous

Prostrate

Glossary for Dwarf Conifers

Aurea: Golden
Compact: Densely growing and more or less round
Conical: Cone-shaped, with a fairly wide base, tapering to a point at the top
Ericoides: Possessing foliage like that of a heather
Fasciate: With foliage tips fused together
Fastigiate: Of erect growth, with branches pointing up
Glaucous: Possessing a whitish, powdery wax
Globose: Globe-shaped
Juvenile foliage: Smaller leaves or needles often carried by young trees
Nana: Latin word for "dwarf"
Pendulous: Hanging down
Plumose: Branches growing randomly up and out, like plumes on a cap
Prostrate: Lying on the ground
Procumbent: Same as Prostrate
Spreading: Tending to grow horizontally
Upright: Higher than wide
Weeping: With branches growing out, then down

Tight and compact, *Picea abies* 'Little Gem' was bred from a witch's broom that appeared on another dwarf spruce, *P. a.* 'Nidiformis', itself the product of a broom. (Photo by John E. Elsley)

onslaughts common to upland regions. Most other tiny conifers are genetic aberrations, the result of mutations that have occurred quite recently or at some point in the past.

A few dwarfs that have become well known were discovered in the wild but under circumstances that indicated they were descendants of a mutated plant long ago. The most famous is the Sargent weeping hemlock, *Tsuga canadensis* 'Pendula', four plants of which are believed to have been found in the Fishkill Mountains of New York more than a century ago. Sargent hemlocks were subsequently propagated so widely that they are now grown all over the world. (Contrary to some belief, incidentally, the plant is named not for Charles Sprague Sargent, the eminent founder of Boston's Arnold Arboretum — although he was given one of the four that were found — but for his cousin Henry Winthrop Sargent, who was a good friend of the discoverer and lived in Fishkill. The anomaly has caused some confusion as Charles Sargent himself discovered a number of other dwarf plants that were later given his name.) Because the environment of the Fishkill Mountains is not punishing enough to cause a plant to grow small to survive, it is assumed that a genetically mutated plant sometime in the past set seed that produced the trees.

Similar events are thought to have resulted in the dwarf Alberta spruce, *Picea glauca* 'Conica', found in the foothills of the Canadian Rockies in 1904 by two botanizers from the Arnold Arboretum, and the very small ground-hugging Cole's prostrate hemlock, *Tsuga canadensis* 'Cole's Prostrate', which nurseryman H. R. Cole came upon in 1929 at the foot of New Hampshire's Mount Madison — in an area where other conifers were experiencing no undue stresses.

One common manifestation of genetic mutation in conifers is the so-called witch's broom, a thickly congested growth mass that may appear at any growing point on a tree and that sometimes does have a broomlike look. The cause is believed to be the abnormal triggering of latent or "adventitious" buds — the kind that, for example, enable a tree to leaf out anew after losing its foliage in a hurricane. On normal trees the latent buds do not develop except in an emergency; but now and then a genetic mishap causes them to burst out in one spot to make a pincushionlike broom. The progeny of such growths — they are usually propagated vegetatively, by cuttings — almost invariably yield dwarfs. Brooms can occur on any kind of tree and indeed have produced dwarf oaks and birches, but they are best known among the conifers precisely because those dwarfs are so prized, and conifer enthusiasts are forever swapping notes on where to find them. Most are only fist-sized but some have been huge: a rare monster once found at the top of a thirty-five-foot tree was six feet high and just as wide.

Some dwarf conifers produced from witch's brooms are stable: they remain dwarfed, and cuttings made from them will produce plants identical to the parent. Some species, however, are characterized by unpredictable behavior, not only occasionally refusing to remain dwarfed but frequently yielding dissimilar offspring. A notorious offender is the Norway spruce, *Picea abies,* which is, as one nurseryman puts it, "promiscuous." It alone has given rise to more than eighty dwarf forms, severely challenging the taxonomists. One popular variety, *Picea abies* 'Little Gem', is a dwarf of a dwarf: little more than a foot high, it comes from a broom found on a *Picea abies* dwarf that was itself produced from a broom.

While witch's brooms are the usual source of genetic dwarfing itself, other mutations can take place that further affect the small plant's appearance. Color shifts are especially common in the dwarf false cypresses and junipers: something happens to the pigmentation process and the foliage may be yellow, or green and yellow, or perhaps even orange. Colors can change with the season, a spring's yellow turning to summer's green. Temperature

Identifying the Conifers

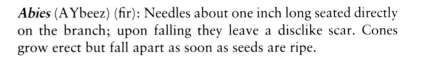

Abies (AYbeez) (fir): Needles about one inch long seated directly on the branch; upon falling they leave a disclike scar. Cones grow erect but fall apart as soon as seeds are ripe.

Cedrus (SEDruss) (cedar): Angular needles about an inch long are scattered on branches but clustered on short spurs that project from the branches. Cones three inches long stand upright on the branches.

Chamaecyparis (KAMeeSIParriss) (false cypress): Scalelike leaves are borne in overlapping pairs on flaring sprays of flattened branchlets.

Cupressus (CooPRESSus) (cypress): Similar to *Chamaecyparis* but leaves are often smaller and branchlets less flattened.

Cryptomeria (CriptoMEERia): Stiff, sharp, four-angled needles occur spirally on the branch and curve back in toward it. Round one-inch cones remain on branches long after seeds have fallen from them. Reddish-brown bark sheds in strips.

Juniperus (JuniPURRus) (juniper): Juvenile leaves are fine and sharply pointed, adult foliage flat and scalelike; but some species present both kinds on the mature plant. Seeds are contained in berries (normally black or bluish-black) that originate like tiny cones.

Picea (PYseeah) (spruce): Short, stiff, angular needles grow all around branchlets, rising from basal pegs (in contrast to *Abies* needles, which have no pegs). Cylindrical cones are pendulous (unlike erect *Abies* cones) and remain hanging from branches for several years.

Pinus (PYnuss) (pine): Needles are long and generally soft to the touch, growing in bundles of two, three, four or five.

Taxus (TAXus) (yew): Dark green needles, flat and about an inch long, are arranged in two ranks on the branch. Seeds are carried in berrylike red cups in the fall.

Thuja (THOOya) (arborvitae): Similar to *Chamaecyparis* in having overlapping pairs of scalelike leaves borne on flat, fan-shaped clusters of branchlets. But their round or egg-shaped cones are much smaller, less than an inch long.

Tsuga (TSOOgah) (hemlock): Small, flat, lustrous needles, generally arranged in two ranks, are paler on underside than above, and grow from cushionlike projections that are nevertheless smaller than *Picea*'s pegs. Cones less than an inch long hang from branches long after seeds have dropped. *Tsuga*'s branches emanate irregularly from the trunk whereas those of *Abies* encircle it regularly.

may be an influence, too: *Pinus strobus* 'Winter Gold' is a dull yellow in winter in warm regions but a bright yellow in colder places. Genetic misplays can also alter the form of the foliage, for example causing a plant's juvenile foliage — the small needles or leaves it bears when young — to remain in one part while the rest of the plant carries adult foliage. Some dwarf cultivars have been deliberately bred to retain the juvenile foliage throughout. A final peculiarity is fasciation: among the cryptomerias especially, the foliage tips can be fused for a while, sprays seemingly glued together. The plant usually outgrows this oddment.

The strange comeuppance that now and then befalls mutated plants, reversion mutation, sometimes affects dwarf conifers. A plant may start exhibiting normal growth patterns amid its dwarfism, or perhaps mutating anew to produce an even weirder look. Oregon nurseryman John Mitsch, a recognized authority on dwarf conifers, has a *Picea abies* cultivar growing by one of his greenhouses that is the offspring of a spruce eighteen inches tall. The offspring is currently more than ten feet high and growing lustily, and it exhibits at least four different kinds of foliage. Mitsch likes to show the tree to visitors, who gaze wonderingly at it as one of nature's pranks.

Dwarf conifers are for the most part not propagated sexually — from seed — but from cuttings or by means of grafting. (Many dwarfs do not often set seed, and in any event a seedling from a mutated plant will in most cases perform normally, thus spoiling the game.) Cuttings of most dwarf conifers are virtually guaranteed to yield plants identical to the parent. Cuttings of a few species, however, notably the pines, the cedars and some of the spruces, require so much time and supervision before rooting reliably that few nurserymen are willing to make the investment. These dwarfs are generally propagated through grafting: a healthy shoot is taken from an existing plant and grafted onto a dwarf rootstock. Other conifers are frequently grafted as well. There is nothing inherently wrong with this procedure, but the buyer of a dwarf conifer should be aware that the unannounced use of a normal rootstock, either by design or by mistake, to support what today surely looks like a dwarf conifer will probably send the plant spurting upward to non-dwarf status in short order. For this reason, among others, it is important to deal with a reputable, knowledgeable nurseryman who buys from trustworthy sources.

The grafting of dwarf conifers has one other aspect: it permits the invention of new forms. At the simplest level it allows for the grafting of a low-growing or pendulous dwarf on top of a rootstock plant whose stem has been trained to grow straight up for a foot or two and is then shorn of its branches; the result puts the dwarf up in the air to create an instant "standard," an umbrella-shaped concoction that can be highly attractive. A favorite subject for such grafting is *Juniperus squamata* 'Blue Star'.

A miniature grove of dwarf conifers decorates Ed Rezek's Malverne, New York, garden. Clockwise from lower left center are, among others, the dark green *Chamaecyparis obtusa* 'Bess'; light blue *Cedrus deodora pygmaea*; yellow-green *Chamaecyparis obtusa lutea nana* and (to the right) a round *Tsuga canadensis* 'Jacqueline Verkade'; beyond are the light green, fastigiate (spiky) *Juniper communis* 'Compressa' and (to the left) a tall, drooping *Chamaecyparis nootkatensis*; just behind the spiky juniper is a fluffy, round *Pinus sylvestris viridis*; to its right, in center, is a small *Chamaecyparis obtusa nana caespetosa* trained as a standard. In the garden's corner in upper left, in front of a large *Actinidia*, is a *Chamaecyparis obtusa* 'Nana Gracilis' trained as a standard, while to its right is a white *Cryptomeria japonica* 'Knaptonensis'. Just to the right of the white lantern is a *Chamaecyparis obtusa contorta*, and to the rear is a weeping *Juniperus scopulurum glauca pendula*; at far right is a light blue *Juniperus squamata* 'Blue Star'. In front of the juniper is a *Thuja occidentalis* 'Rhineglow' trained and grafted by Rezek to form three pompoms. In lower right is a *Chamaecyparis obtusa* 'Elf'. At center bottom is another Rezek graft, a small round *Chamaecyparis pisifera* 'White Knight' on top of a *Chamaecyparis obtusa* 'Lutea Nana', while immediately back of it is a conical *Picea glauca* 'Sanders Blue'. The two flowering shrubs in lower right are New Guinea impatiens. (Photo by Edward F. Rezek)

Another quite common practice is to make a low-growing, spreading plant by using as the scion (upper section) of the graft one or two lower branches from an otherwise upright dwarf tree. The lower branches of conifers, it seems, are genetically programmed to continue growing outward even when nothing is growing above them, rather than altering their behavior and heading upward; under normal circumstances they will not make a new central leader, and it is presumed that a horizontally shaped dwarf conifer so created will remain so. Purchasers of what seem to be horizontal dwarfs are well advised, however, to find out from the nurseryman whether the tree is a natural spreader or has been fashioned by grafting. For now and then such trees will play the reversion game and abruptly establish a new leader far out at the end of a branch, producing a look that is distinctly odd. In any event, anyone owning such a tree should be on the lookout for any vertical growths and prune them out immediately.

For those who want something novel, grafting opens the door to any number of unusual effects. The Oregon nurseryman Jean Iseli, who carried on a flourishing wholesale trade in both dwarf and normal conifers, took to producing on a large scale plants that are grafted in unexpected ways. He called them Dantsugi plants, as the practice is an adaptation of an old Japanese technique wherein grafts are used to create odd designs, but his Dantsugis defied all traditions. He even grafted three different *Picea abies* cultivars on one rootstock, getting a plant with three dissimilar foliages, and he was not above combining foliages of different colors on one plant. There seem to be no limits to the possibilities along this provocative line.

It is not necessary, however, to go beyond conventionally produced dwarf conifers to obtain effects that are both unorthodox and felicitous. The soft, grass-green foliage of the dwarf Alberta spruce (*Picea glauca* 'Conica') presents itself on a dense conical bush so perfectly shaped it seems turned on a lathe; a similar lushness can be seen in the dwarf deodar cedar (*Cedrus deodara* 'Nana'). At the other extreme, some of the small pines manage to make prickliness seem distinctly stylish. And prostrate dwarfs like *Picea abies* 'Procumbens' or 'Cole's Prostrate' hemlock can make a carpet more complete than any ground cover. They will even trail over a retaining wall — imagine a tree that grows downward. Although the dwarf Nootka cypress (*Chamaecyparis nootkatensis* 'Pendula') is not a typical "weeper," its foliage droops arrestingly; and one of the Hinoki cypresses, *Chamaecyparis obtusa* 'Kosteri', exhibits fans of foliage that may twist one way or another in a unique manner. And although some *Picea abies* cultivars may be oddly formed, some of the dwarfs of the American white pine *(Pinus strobus)* are especially — and entertainingly — contorted.

For the practical-minded it should be pointed out that dwarf conifers have long been used to solve some humble but very real problems both in gardens and elsewhere. Designers of suburban shopping malls would be hard put to find more useful plants to anchor earthen slopes and divide parking areas than the tough dwarf junipers, which can be seen everywhere. And with modern homes increasingly being constructed bereft of noticeable stone foundations, dwarf conifers of every type are being used more and more for the equivalent of foundation planting: unless the homeowner remains for more than one generation the plants are not likely to rise up to block the view.

In choosing dwarf conifers either for the home garden or for other situations it can be useful to visit botanical gardens or arboretums that grow such plants so as to get an idea of relative sizes, shapes and textures. Then make a preliminary judgment as to what kinds of plants you might want to seek out. Although the list at the end of this chapter suggests some well-known varieties or cultivars, they may not satisfy your needs — and they may also be unavailable. But a reputable nursery owner (for a list of a few suggested ones, see the Appendix, or write to the American Conifer Society, whose address is on page 186) may well have new cultivars equal or superior to those listed. When you get around to visiting the nursery or garden center itself you will probably want to have the eventual location of the tree (or trees) in mind. Placing dwarf conifers in the garden is, of course, a totally personal matter. One general rule is nevertheless worth observing: plants intended for the crest of a small hill or rockery, or even for just below the crest, should not be upright growers — better stick with horizontal or pendulous plants for such spots. One other note: dwarf conifers of varying shapes and textures can make delightful combinations all by themselves. For more design thoughts, see chapter 12.

Conifers for the most part demand considerable sunlight, although they are not likely to do well if planted near a wall that heats up in summer. Hemlocks alone prefer shade to open sunlight, while yews and some of the junipers will probably flourish either with sun or without it. Some of the false cypresses *(Chamaecyparis)* are vulnerable to strong winds. For specific advice on these matters, inquire at your nursery.

Knowledgeable nursery personnel should be able to estimate a dwarf conifer's likely growth rate. Guessing its "eventual" height is a trickier question, for in theory most dwarfs simply continue to grow (though at a ponderously slow rate) until they are the size of a normal tree. To simplify matters the nursery industry has invoked the "useful life" concept. What most gardeners and homeowners want, they reason, is a tree that will suffice for a dozen to fifteen years; after that the owners will have moved, or chosen a substitute plant, or thought up another use for the space. Height estimates are thus conventionally given for the twelve- to fifteen-year span.

Most dwarf conifers, like their full-sized counterparts, are hardy to the

The dwarf *Pinus strobus,* or eastern white pine, exhibits a beguiling softness. (Photo by Michael Carlebach)

coldest areas of the United States. Of the basic eleven genera, only the cedars and cypresses are marginal; and of course California's redwoods and giant sequoias have difficulty in colder climates. Nurseries will probably stock only plants suitable for their particular hardiness zone (see hardiness map, page 26), but bear in mind that elevation and other special geographical factors can affect a plant's resistance to cold.

Typical garden soil, especially if it is well drained, will suit most of the conifers, but a special kind of reverse admonition is in order here. Because a major object of owning dwarf plants is to keep them that way, they should not be given soil that is overly rich in nutrients lest they respond with unwelcome vigor. Similarly, fertilizers are not needed unless you are looking for extra growth to fulfill some special need.

Increasingly today dwarf conifers are not only grown by the producing nursery in containers but sold that way too. Transplanting them into the garden thereby requires special procedures. For in contrast to larger trees, which will have been transplanted from time to time before being balled-and-burlapped for shipment, their roots thus having been spurred to put out new growth, the dwarf's roots will have become so accustomed to the container that if simply dropped into a newly dug hole they may stay within

Typical of the strange shapes offered by some dwarf conifers is this *Picea pungens* 'Glauca Prostrata'. (Photo by Harold E. Greer)

their confines and not send out new feeders. First, therefore, dig a hole at least four times the size of the container, returning half the soil back into the hole while adjusting it for friability (to loosen heavy soil, add sand or perlite; to make light soil more friable add peat moss). Second, remove the plant from the container and pull its roots away from the soil; you may even want to "distress" them by scratching with a gardening claw. Then place the plant in the hole, making sure the roots lead off into the new soil, add the remaining soil and tamp down thoroughly to remove any air pockets. (See drawings page 43).

The newly planted dwarf should of course be well watered at the outset, and to be on the safe side should be given at least an inch of water every week for the first summer and fall. Apply water additionally during hot spells and droughts, and wet the foliage with a hose spray. Thereafter it should not be necessary to water except during extreme summer heat or drought.

Generally disease-free, dwarf conifers may occasionally attract aphids and other minor pests; if the intruders cannot be flushed off with the hose, apply a systemic insecticide (being sure to follow it up with a second treatment in a couple of weeks). The only other maintenance concern is pruning. Being such slow growers, the plants will rarely need cutting back of any kind. Some of the compact, dense cultivars nevertheless can become cluttered with dead growth in their interiors, and this should be removed if it becomes too thick — one experienced practitioner recommends doing so by subjecting the plant's insides to a heavy water spray. If any meticulous shaping of the plant is needed, the same practitioner has just the tool to recommend: nail scissors.

U.S. DEPARTMENT OF AGRICULTURE HARDINESS ZONE MAP

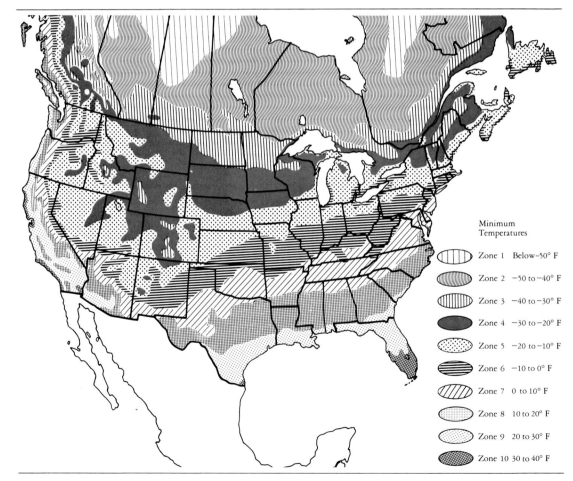

Minimum
Temperatures

Zone 1   Below−50° F

Zone 2   −50 to −40° F

Zone 3   −40 to −30° F

Zone 4   −30 to −20° F

Zone 5   −20 to −10° F

Zone 6   −10 to 0° F

Zone 7   0 to 10° F

Zone 8   10 to 20° F

Zone 9   20 to 30° F

Zone 10 30 to 40° F

A Sampling of Dwarf Conifers

(H or W = height or width after twelve to fifteen years. Z = lowest hardiness zone.)

ABIES (fir) — Native to cool mountainous areas, most firs may suffer from warm summer temperatures. But their delicate beauty earns them a place in most conifer gardens.

> *Abies alba,* silver fir. From central and southern Europe. *A. a.* 'Compacta' is a slow-growing shrub with upright branchlets. H 1–2′ Z3

> *A. balsamea,* balsam fir. Denizen of the White Mountains and other high regions in the Northeast. *A. b.* 'Nana' is a dense round-topped shrub with dark green (but sometimes blue-gray) foliage. H 12″ Z3

CEDRUS (cedar) — Graceful trees originally from the Mediterranean and the Himalayas.

> *Cedrus deodara,* deodar cedar. Native to the Himalayas, with needle-like leaves up to two inches long. *C. d.* 'Aurea Pendula' is a drooping or prostrate cultivar, sometimes with golden-green foliage. H 18″ Z6

> *C. libani,* cedar of Lebanon. From Asia Minor, and characterized by bright or dark green foliage. *C. l.* 'Minuta' is extremely dwarf with tiny needles. H 18″ Z5

CHAMAECYPARIS (false cypress) — Three species *(lawsoniana, nootkatensis* and *thyoides)* are North American; the rest are from Japan and Taiwan. Easy to grow and thus highly popular, the false cypresses offer a wide variety of sizes and shapes to choose from. Some, however, are unpredictable in their growth habits, and most are vulnerable to heat.

> *Chamaecyparis lawsoniana,* Lawson cypress. Originally from southwestern Oregon and the northern California coast, these plants are especially noted for their color variations. *C. l.* 'Ellwoodi' is slender and spirelike with blue-green or blue foliage (H 34″), while *C. l.* 'Minima', which is globose when young and then conical, bears yellowish-green leaves (H 18″). *C. l.* 'Filiformis Compacta' is a globular bush with blue-green, threadlike foliage (H 18″ W 30″). Z 5–6

C. nootkatensis, Nootka cypress. From the northwest coast. *C. n.* 'Glauca Compacta' is compact with glaucous (tinged with white) needles. H 3' Z4

C. obtusa, Hinoki cypress. Japan. The globose *C. o.* 'Kosteri' has elegantly twisted dark green foliage (H 3'), while the less regularly globose 'Nana Gracilis' is covered with cup-shaped sprays (H 30"). Z5

C. pisifera, Sawara cypress. A Japanese species with particularly remarkable foliage. The globular *C. p.* 'Plumosa Compressa' has gold-tipped leaves (H 9–12"), while *C. p.* 'Snow' is a fuzzy white (H 12–15"). Z5

C. thyoides, white cedar. This species is from swampy areas of the eastern United States. *C. t.* 'Andelyensis' is a slender conical plant with gray-green foliage. H 3' Z3

CRYPTOMERIA (sometimes called Japanese cedar) — Some of this genus's dwarfs bear foliage that turns bronze or blue in the winter. The tree originates from Japan.

Cryptomeria japonica, cryptomeria or Japanese cedar. Noted for retaining its juvenile foliage (sharp in-curved needles) into maturity. *C. j.* 'Vilmoriniana' is a globose dwarf with rich dense green foliage that turns reddish-bronze in winter (H 15–18"), while *C. j.* 'Elegans Nana' is wider than high and particularly hardy. 'Vilmoriniana' is hardy to Z5, 'Elegans Nana' to Z4.

CUPRESSUS (the true cypress) — A highly attractive plant for gardeners in warmer regions.

Cupressus glabra, dwarf Arizona cypress. Native to the southwestern United States. *C. g.* 'Compacta' is a tight conical globe with glaucous foliage. H 18" Z6

JUNIPERUS (juniper) — Found in their native state all over the world, the junipers are particularly characterized by odd combinations of juvenile and adult foliage. Many of these tough plants are multistemmed and thus shrubs. The most popular dwarfs are horizontal growers.

Juniperus chinensis, Chinese juniper. Native to the Far East. *J. c.* 'Pfitzeriana' is a wide spreader with gray-green needles. H 3' W 9', but may spread much farther. Z4

J. communis, common juniper. Europe, northern Asia and North America. *J. c.* 'Berkshire' is a very slow-growing bun with silvery-blue foliage (H 9–12″), while *J. c.* 'Hornibrookii' is a spreader with layered branches carrying white-tipped foliage (H 2′ W 6–7′). Z3

J. horizontalis, creeping juniper. North America. *J. h.* 'Blue Chip' is a spreading but compact plant with bright blue foliage (H 12–15″ W 6–7′), while *J. c.* 'Wiltoni', the "blue rug juniper," is equally blue but a prostrate grower (H 4″ W 8–10′). Z3

J. sabina, savin juniper. From Europe, east to Siberia. Another low grower. *J. s.* 'Buffalo' has soft, bright green foliage (H 12″ W 7–8′), while *J. s.* 'Tamariscifolia' is blue-green (H 15–18″ W 7–9′). Z3

J. squamata. From the Far East, and noted for cultivars with prostrate growth. *J. s.* 'Blue Carpet' is outstanding for its silver-blue foliage, which remains juvenile; a wide spreader (H 12–15″ W 9–12′); *J. s.* 'Blue Star' is also attractive and spreads less. Z4

LARIX (larch) — The best-known deciduous conifer. Its lacy, pinelike leaves may turn a rich golden-yellow in the fall before dropping.

Larix x eurolepsis, Dunkeld larch. Originated in Scotland, this hybrid is remarkably free of diseases that attack other larches and bears decorative reddish cones. The dwarf form, *L. e.* 'Varied Directions', is a weeper. H 18–24″ Z2

PICEA (spruce) — A broad genus mostly from Asia and North America but with one prominent species from Europe — the Norway spruce. The dwarf varieties, though mostly very attractive, are characterized by considerable genetic instability.

Picea abies, Norway spruce. Northern and central Europe. *P. a.* 'Nidiformis' is a low, dense, spreading shrub with a nestlike depression in its center (H 2′ W 4′); a sport, from a 'Nidiformis' witch's broom, has yielded *P. a.* 'Little Gem', the most diminutive spruce of all. *P. a.* 'Procumbens' makes a creeping mound with branches heaping up (H 3′ W 3′). Z3

P. glauca, white spruce. Native to Canada and the eastern United States, the species is most noted for *P. g.* 'Conica', the conical dwarf Alberta spruce with its fine soft grass-green foliage. H 6′ Z3

P. omorika, Serbian spruce. Eastern Europe. A dependable species known for its bicolored needles, green on top and blue below. *P. o.* 'Nana' is a generally pyramidal dwarf slightly wider than high. H 3′ Z4

P. pungens, Colorado spruce. From the western United States, and known for its sharp, one-inch-long blue-green needles. The subspecies *P. p. glauca* has foliage that is still bluer. Two dwarfs are choice: *P. p. g.* 'Globosa', which is a dense round shrub (H 2'), and the weeping *P. p. g.* 'Pendula' (H 18"). Z3

PINUS (pine) — A genus found all over the Northern Hemisphere from the Arctic to the tropics and possessing a large number of dwarf forms.

Pinus densiflora, Japanese red pine. Japan. The full-sized tree has a tendency to twist and knot and is thus favored by bonsai devotees. The dwarf *P. d.* 'Pendula' is a weeper that trails handsomely over rocks (H and W depend on culture), while *P. d.* 'Umbraculifera', the Tanyosho or "umbrella" pine, is generally vase-shaped (H 3'). Z4

P. mugo, mountain pine. From the Alps and other European mountains. *P. m.* (Iseli) 'White Bud' is a compact dark green dwarf. H 2' Z2

P. strobus, eastern white pine. From the northeastern United States and eastern Canada. The dwarf forms exhibit a lovely softness in springtime when their new growth appears. *P. s.* 'Nana' is a spreading mound with bluish-green needles. H 3' Z3

P. sylvestris, Scots pine. From Eurasia. Another species producing odd dwarf forms. *P. s.* 'Mitsch's Weeping' bears green, twisted, pendulous branches (H and W depend on culture). More conventional in habit is the spreader *P. s.* 'Saxatilis' (H 6" W 20"). Z3

TAXUS (yew) — Evergreen shrubs and small trees from Europe and Japan, long recommended for planting around homes.

Taxus baccata, English yew. Although some dwarf yews have a tendency to grow too fast, one worth trying is *T. b.* 'Argentea Minor', a spreader whose dark green leaves are edged in yellow in spring, in silver later (H 15"); *T. b.* 'Repandens' with its unvariegated dark green foliage spreads less (H 15–20"). Z6

THUJA (arborvitae) — From North America and the Far East. It is another genus whose dwarfs may combine juvenile with adult foliage, and the results are often striking. Many forms possess unusual color, which is enhanced if the tree is planted in moist soil with afternoon shade.

Thuja occidentalis, American arborvitae. The pyramidal *T. o.* 'Ericoides' has heatherlike foliage green in summer but turning reddish-violet in winter (H 2'), while *T. o.* 'Rheingold', also pyramidal, keeps its juvenile foliage, which is golden or bronze (H 3′). *T. o.* 'Emerald', while not so dwarf (H 3–4′), keeps its bright green foliage in winter. Z4

T. orientalis, Oriental arborvitae. Native to China and Korea. *T. o.* 'Minima Glauca' is a small globular bush whose foliage — glaucous green in summer, yellow-brown in winter — presents itself in vertical sprays. H 2′ Z6

TSUGA (hemlock) — A handsome genus native to North America and also to the Far East, with innumerable dwarf forms.

Tsuga canadensis, Canadian hemlock. By far the best-known species. *T. c.* 'Minuta' is one of the smallest varieties (H 3″). *T. c.* 'Bennett' is a flat-topped spreader presenting symmetrical layers of foliage (H 18″). *T. c.* 'Cole's Prostrate' (sometimes listed as 'Prostrata') lies flat on the ground (H 12″ W 4′ or more). *T. c.* 'Pendula' is the famed Sargent weeping hemlock, which actually is large for a dwarf (H 10′ or more). Z4

3

Rhododendrons and Azaleas

FOR THOSE WHO HAVE BEEN PRIVILEGED to view it, the sight of virtually limitless expanses of dwarf rhododendrons in bloom in their remote, mountainous native habitat is overwhelming.

"Now for the first time," wrote the British plant explorer Captain F. Kingdon-Ward on a visit to the 10,000-foot-high alpine moorland of the Himalayas early in this century, "we gaze across square miles of rock and Rhododendron, and not much else, the swirling colors of pygmy Lapponicums, Saluenenses, aromatic Anthopogons and bubbling Campylogynums making a never-to-be-forgotten picture; the whole Rhododendron sea is flecked with shimmering foam, sulphur, apricot, salmon, Tyrian purple, violet. On the sheltered side of the valley the Neriiflorums in their various crouching attitudes glow blood red against the irregular patches of snow."

Captain Kingdon-Ward was glimpsing the source land of the great preponderance of the smaller rhododendron species that have been discovered to date, and that can bring so much beauty and distinction to the small-scale garden. The source region is an arc encompassing the high Himalayan country from northern India through Tibet, Nepal, Sikkim and Bhutan and into southwest China. On the lower slopes grow the larger species with their bigger leaves and opulent blossoms, but as the altitude increases the rhododendrons become smaller — until in the remote upland passes the ground is

OPPOSITE: Rich red blossoms adorn a prostrate dwarf azalea, *Rhododendron nakaharai* 'Mount Seven Star', at the Martha's Vineyard growing area of the discerning horticulturist Polly Hill. (Photo by Pamela Harper)

carpeted with an extraordinary profusion of dwarfs little more than a foot or so high, which, like all rhododendrons, bloom in the spring or early summer of the year.

Other dwarf rhododendron species come from the mountains of Taiwan, Korea and Japan — which also furnish most of the dwarf azaleas, members of the greater rhododendron genus. The remaining few are found in the great south Asian archipelago stretching from Sumatra to New Guinea, and in the southern Appalachians in the United States. It is these elegant, diminutive but extravagantly blooming plants that, in either species or hybrid form, are increasingly being acquired by rock gardeners and other small-garden enthusiasts all across the United States. These devotees hope to reproduce, if only on a minute scale, some of the glory witnessed by Kingdon-Ward.

The kind of environment that gives rise to luxuriant natural sweeps of rhododendrons and azaleas, particularly the dwarf varieties, is worth noting. It is high, cool and moist. The Himalayas are monsoon country, washed periodically by heavy rains and refreshed at other times by mists; the other habitats are similarly blessed. Summers are rarely hot, and while winters are bitterly cold the land tends to be covered by snows that keep ground-level temperatures from dropping much below the mid-twenties. The combination of low temperatures and high rainfall slows the action of soil microorganisms, so that the soil is rich in organic matter and on the acid side. It is also coarse and thus well drained.

Such conditions are quite specialized, and indeed the truly ideal garden surroundings for rhododendrons and azaleas are found only in limited parts of the United States, most notably the coastal sections of the Pacific Northwest with their moderate maritime climate (the British Isles and parts of the European continent are also fortunate). But gardeners in other areas can grow a great many of these gems successfully if they observe certain precautions, and hybridizing has also immensely expanded the number of plants that can be enjoyed in less benign climates. The history of rhododendron and azalea culture, in fact, can be largely seen as the continuing effort by hybridizers to expand the horticultural limits of these handsome and flamboyantly flowering plants.

The hybridizers do have a stupendous range of material to work with. The genus — part of the family of ericaceous or heath plants — contains more than nine hundred species, of which perhaps a fourth are dwarf or semidwarf. Rhododendrons can be considered dwarf if they can be expected to grow no higher than two feet in ten years, while those attaining three or four feet may be deemed semidwarf.

Botanists generally divide the rhododendron genus into three main groups: the lepidotes, the elepidotes and the azaleas. The actual botanical

difference between the first two groups is minor — the lepidotes have infin-
itesimal scales on the undersides of their leaves while the elepidotes do not
("e" meaning "without") — but it is vital, for the two are almost completely
exclusive and are quite difficult to interbreed. Luckily there are so many
species in each group that the exclusivity matters little. The lepidotes' leaves
are small, usually no more than an inch long and often tinier; because of
this characteristic you can spot a lepidote instantly from way off. Many of
the dwarfs are lepidotes, their high-country domain not demanding the large
moisture-holding leaves of the elepidotes.

Another difference between the two: the underside of many elepidote
leaves, while bereft of scales, is covered with a soft, fuzzy substance called
indumentum, which may be brownish but can alternatively be orange or
even red, and which is greatly admired by rhododendron buffs, who are
forever turning leaves over to fondle them. If you turn a rhododendron leaf
over and find it without indumentum, it is probably a lepidote (though there
are many exceptions); take out a magnifying glass and you can probably
identify the scales.

The smallness of the lepidotes' leaves admittedly can make them difficult
to distinguish from the azaleas, all of whose leaves are small and without
indumentum. Like the elepidotes, the azaleas have no scales (actually they
are botanically included with the elepidotes); but they do generally have
small appressed (i.e. flattened) hairs growing on their leaves, especially along
the midrib of the undersurface; no rhododendrons have such hairs. The
subtlety of these differences can confound even an expert. "Sometimes,"
remarks one azalea authority, "there's nothing to do but count the stamens." There she is on fairly solid ground, at least during the blooming
season. Almost all azaleas have five lobes to the flower, and most have only
one stamen for each lobe, or five in all; most rhododendrons have two
stamens per lobe and at least five lobes, for a total of ten or more stamens.

In the wintertime, to be sure, the identification problem can be simpler,
for while most rhododendrons are evergreen, many azaleas are deciduous.
That is scant help in the case of the dwarfs, however: almost all of the dwarf
azaleas are evergreen.

The small stature of both dwarf rhododendrons and dwarf azaleas is
almost entirely brought about environmentally, in response to the rigors of
their alpine habitat. As with the conifers, they can be subject to sudden
genetic mutations: witch's brooms have been found on many, although little
has been done in using these to produce new forms. The one clear-cut
genetic factor is variation in size within one species, the result of gradual
genetic adaptations to specific environments. Thus there are both dwarf
forms and larger forms of *Rhododendron racemosum,* a popular pink-
blooming species from China's Yunnan and Szechwan provinces that is

Blossoming dwarf rhododendrons, none more than two feet high, crowd the testing area maintained by Warren Berg, a retired 747 pilot who conducts a thriving hybridizing program on Washington's Olympic Peninsula. In lower left is a white *Rhododendron yakusimanum* crossed with *R. tsariense;* another and larger *R. yakusimanum x R. tsariense* is beyond it. Left of the *yakusimanum* is a pink 'Ginny Gee', bred by Berg, while beyond 'Ginny Gee' is a yellow 'Patty Bee', another Berg hybrid, and beyond those are two other Berg crosses. In center rear, just coming into bloom, are one or two yellow or cream-colored *R. keiskei* 'Yaku Fairy'; in front of them are Berg's large yellow 'Golden Bee' and a small yellow *R. keiskei*. At far right is a red-blossoming 'Moonstone' x 'Carmen', and beyond it a pink 'Ginny Gee' sister plant. (Photo by Warren Berg)

Blossoms totally obscure 'Wigeon', a new hybrid dwarf rhododendron.
(Photo by Harold E. Greer)

much used in hybridizing; the smaller forms come from higher elevations. Those who have seen *R. racemosum* growing wild report that it blooms from February to October in the Chinese mountains, filling the upland slopes with magnificent swaths of rosy pink.

In the West, the earliest rhododendrons brought into cultivation — in the seventeenth and eighteenth centuries — were from the European Alps or neighboring ranges; some were dwarfs. Toward the end of the eighteenth century, plants began to be imported into England from two other key sources, Asia Minor and America. Those from Asia Minor were beautiful but tender; the American species, notably *R. catawbiense* from North Carolina, were perhaps less graceful but vastly tougher, capable of withstanding temperatures far below zero degrees Fahrenheit.

With the subsequent addition of even more colorful species from the Himalayan region — which despite their high source area were not very hardy, being accustomed to winter snow cover — the first successful hybridizing efforts got under way in England in the mid-nineteenth century. These endeavors brought together the lovely Asians with the hardy Americans to yield handsome, stalwart plants that became known as "ironclads" for their ability to survive icy blasts. (Many ironclads based on those early crosses are still sold today in both Europe and the United States.) These were all large plants; no popular hybrid dwarfs were produced at that time. But the key principle was established: cross a tender Asian plant with a cold-resistant American and you have something that large numbers of gardeners can grow with pleasure and success.

So it was that when the first successfully hardy dwarf rhododendron hybrids were brought out in this century the same idea was invoked. By that time a group of hardy dwarf species had been found in the southeastern United States, in particular *R. carolinianum,* from the mountains of Tennessee and the Carolinas. One of the great rhododendron hybridizers of the last half century, Guy Nearing, crossed it with *R. fastigiatum* (from Yunnan) in the 1940s to produce both 'Ramapo' and 'Purple Gem', two light purple or violet dwarfs that have become mainstays of the specialty nursery trade. Another celebrated cross, *R. carolinianum* with *R. dauricum* (from eastern Siberia), was made in 1940 by Edmund Mezitt of Massachusetts and resulted in 'PJM', a lavender-flowering semidwarf that continues to sell well in frosty northeastern areas. "I'd say that just about all these plants," Connecticut nurseryman John Oliver remarks, gesturing to his wide selection of dwarf rhododendrons suitable to southern New England, "have that Carolina blood in them."

Concerns about hardiness barely bother the rhododendron fanciers of the Pacific Northwest, who can grow most of the tender species and hybrids with only passing attention to frost damage. But hybridizers there, as elsewhere, are constantly bringing forth new dwarf plants that boast unusual flowers or foliage, and some of their crosses have also proved quite hardy in the bargain. One of these breeders is Warren Berg of Port Ludlow, Washington, whose yellow-blooming 'Patty Bee' has withstood temperatures of minus 10 degrees Fahrenheit on the East Coast. In its case the hardiness is contributed by *R. keiskei* 'Yaku Fairy', a cultivar of a dwarf species from a mountaintop on an island south of Japan ('Yaku Fairy' is itself a newly popular selection of the species). Berg, a retired 747 pilot — who also keeps bees for pollinating purposes and so uses "Bee" in most of the names he confers — has traveled several times to the Orient on plant-hunting expeditions and has brought back a number of valuable new varieties with which to experiment. Other plant explorers have similarly added to the storehouse of species and varieties from the Himalayas and elsewhere as recently as the early 1980s, further enlarging the opportunities for hybridizers in the future.

In the case of dwarf azaleas, no dependably hardy species has ever been found with the ironclad characteristics of the tough American rhododendrons. Yet a handful of species from Japan and Taiwan that have been proven moderately hardy — certainly to Zone 7 and very often to most of Zone 6 — have long intrigued hybridizers in both Japan and the United States. Two of them, *R. indicum* and *R. eriocarpum,* have for generations been interbred by the Japanese to produce what are known as the Satsuki azaleas. These pleasing dwarfs unfortunately are not dependably hardy in the colder parts of the United States. But the same two species as well as others from Japan were interbred several decades ago by Benjamin Morrison, director of the National Arboretum in Washington, D.C., to produce the famed Glenn Dale azaleas, some of which were dwarfs and moderately hardy. More recently, Robert Gartrell of Wyckoff, New Jersey, has by careful experimentation taken the Satsukis one step further toward hardiness with his small Robin Hill azaleas, many of which bloom late — in June and July — in attractive pastel tones.

Another dwarf azalea species, found on Taiwan but utilized in plant breeding by the Japanese, has proven the hardiest to date. It is *R. nakaharai*, which the Japanese hybridizer Tsuneshige Rokujo has used to breed a series of late-blooming, prostrate plants that are truly astonishing. For the United States market Dr. Rokujo (he is a former surgeon) sends seeds to Polly Hill, a supremely proficient amateur who gardens in North Tisbury, Massachusetts, on Martha's Vineyard; Mrs. Hill in turn selects the most promising, names them and introduces them to the trade. Her North Tisbury azaleas are certifiably hardy to Zone 6 and wondrous to behold. Generally growing no higher than a foot to fifteen inches, they creep out eventually to cover an area thirty or forty inches in diameter (a few have spread eight or ten feet), taking root as they go, and put out a carpet of vivid red, pink, salmon-colored or white blossoms in June, July and even into August, right down there on the ground.

The late blooming is arguably the most attractive feature of these dwarf azaleas (and some of the rhododendrons), and some theorists have speculated that it may be due to the plants' ancestors having become accustomed to emerging late in the season from their snow cover. It is truly a boon to the small-scale gardener, indeed to all horticulturists. "There used to be nothing like this in bloom after early June," says Polly Hill. "Now we have something that puts on a good show in the summer, not only for the people who have summer places but for those who don't go away but want a succession of bloom wherever they are."

R. nakaharai itself is available from certain specialty nurseries in the United States, as are many other rhododendron and azalea species. As with so many other kinds of plants, there is a slight separation between the species aficionados and those who collect the hybrids. The species admirers — whose numbers are admittedly small — claim that their plants represent, as one of them put it, "the clean efficiency of nature in its most appealing aspect," superlatively integrating structure and blossom. Hybrids, of course, not only extend the range of the genus and thus make possible the growing of a far greater number of plants; they are generally more tractable and

The small, strikingly handsome *Rhododendron yakusimanum,* little more than eighteen inches high at maturity, was first imported into the United States from Japan in the 1950s and is now much favored by collectors and hybridizers alike. Only its expensiveness, caused by the long time required for propagation, prevents it and other slow-growing dwarfs from becoming big sellers. (Photo by John E. Elsley)

bloom more luxuriantly. Gardeners interested in collecting species may want to consider becoming members of the Rhododendron Species Foundation, a nonprofit organization south of Seattle, which grows most of the plants (including azalea species) and sells clones to its members. (For information write the RSF at P.O. Box 3798, Federal Way, WA 98063-3798.) For a list of specialty nurseries retailing both species and choice hybrids, see the Appendix.

Whichever kind you grow — and although purists might argue for planting only one kind, there's really no reason not to mix them — there will be the ever-present question of hardiness. It is the number one issue among

Resembling small roses, pink blossoms burst forth on *R. indicum*
'Balsaminaeflorum', a species azalea. (Photo by Harold E. Greer)

rhododendron and azalea growers. The difficulty is that much more than
minimum winter cold is involved. Other factors include the speed with
which that cold arrives, its duration, the possibility of winter thaws, and,
above all, summer heat. Recall the Himalayan environment: it is one where
winter arrives gradually, so that plants have a chance to harden off. Ironi-
cally, in the colder areas of the midwestern United States and in the Northeast it is often the early October frosts that are lethal rather than the zero
readings of midwinter. "Plants that can take twenty below in February,"
says John Oliver, "can't take twenty above in October." When subzero
readings do arrive, plants may survive if the mercury stays down for only
one night; but a five-day stretch will finish them. Conversely, a midwinter
thaw can be ruinous to some rhododendron plants as it will induce them to
break dormancy — so that when cold returns their buds will be badly dam-

aged. So complex is the question of rhododendrons' resistance to cold that many nurserymen say the term "hardiness" should be replaced by "adaptability." A plant that is listed as hardy to minus 10 degrees in the Northwest often proves far less hardy in the East as it cannot adapt to the abrupt temperature swings.

Finally there is the heat of summer. Many a plant will make it through the winter only to wither in July's hot, dry days. The farther south one goes, the greater the risk — and rhododendrons are more vulnerable in this regard than azaleas. Skillful mulching and judicious watering can often ward off the peril, but many species and hybrids are simply not geared for prolonged hot spells. To some extent hybridizers have been able to increase their plants' adaptability by selecting out those seedlings that endure and then using them to hybridize further, but there are limits. All the more reason to purchase plants only from reputable specialty concerns that are familiar with the plants' capabilities as well as growing conditions in your area, including its climatic perils. If you want to try plants that are on the edge of hardiness — and many gardeners find a zest in responding to that challenge — you will at least have the facts in hand.

The key word is protection, against freezing winds and hot sunlight, and against drying out. Dwarfs can be shielded from the wind by being planted next to or between large rocks, or in the lee of a hedge or row of trees or large shrubs. They can be guarded against the hottest sun by being planted on a north-facing slope, by the presence of shade trees pruned high or by a lath structure. Contrary to popular belief, rhododendrons and azaleas are not true shade plants, for the absence of sun makes them leggy while good light keeps them compact. They do need protection from the hot midday sun, however. Above all it is the roots, which grow near the surface, that need shielding against heat and drying; the answer is a good ground cover, or better yet a substantial, permanent mulch.

Almost as important is a porous soil. Again, remember those alpine conditions: moisture descends frequently but sluices away readily. The plants cannot stand wet feet — if they become water-logged they will almost certainly develop root rot. Soil should have a high humus content, which can be achieved through ample helpings of bark, peat moss or leaf mold. Such additives will also help keep the soil on the acid side; a pH rating between 4 and 5.5 is ideal. You might want also to find out whether your water tends toward an alkaline or acid rating; if it is alkaline, you will want to add ferrous sulphate (not aluminum sulphate, which is toxic to these plants) to the rhododendrons' or azaleas' soil from time to time. In most cases it will not be necessary to add lime.

The same admonitions that apply to planting conifers govern putting members of the rhododendron genus in the ground: dig a hole at least four times the diameter of the root ball, and scar or "distress" the roots after removing them from the container. Two extra admonitions are in order, however. First, mix peat moss or leaf mold into the soil that will go back into the hole, even if the soil is already acid enough. Second, make sure the root ball ends up at the same level as the surrounding soil or even slightly above. Water must not be allowed to puddle around the stems, and the surface roots — vital to the plants' health — must remain near the surface.

SUCCESSFUL PLANTING

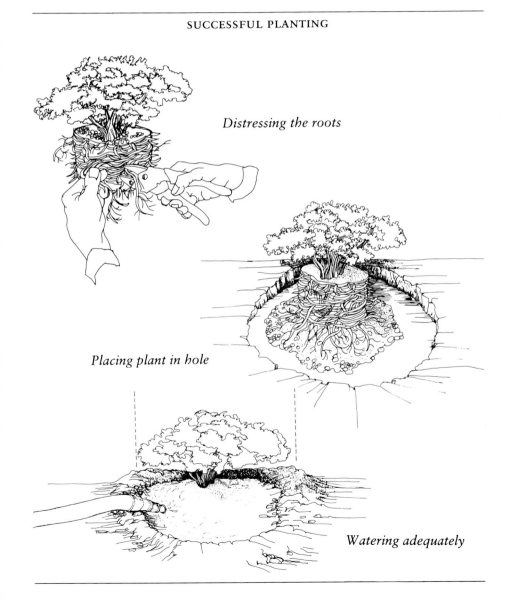

Distressing the roots

Placing plant in hole

Watering adequately

The pure white flowers of *Rhododendron* 'Dora Amateis', emerging from pink buds, combine with deep green foliage for an attractive show each spring. Like many other popular hybrids, 'Dora Amateis' owes its toughness to having been bred from *R. carolinianum*, a dwarf from the southeastern United States. (Photo by John E. Elsley)

Mulching is mandatory, and should be maintained throughout the year at a depth of two or three inches: a good mulch helps keep the soil cool and moist in summer and minimizes the effects of temperature swings in winter. Shredded oak leaves are good (if they are not shredded, six to eight inches will be needed), as are pine or other evergreen needles; other materials include buckwheat hulls, pine or fir bark, even peanut hulls or ground corn cobs. Do not use peat moss as a mulch (it cakes on the surface), or tobacco stems or cocoa bean hulls (they are toxic to these plants). Once the mulch is in place, do not disturb it except to renew periodically; do not under any circumstances cultivate the soil.

A generous organic mulch will also go far toward providing whatever food your rhododendrons and azaleas need. Some nurseries recommend outright fertilizing as well, especially the first year — but be sure to exercise

Rhododendron 'Purple Gem', hybridized by the late Guy Nearing, is fully hardy to temperatures below zero Fahrenheit. Similar to it is another Nearing favorite called 'Ramapo'. (Photo by John E. Elsley)

restraint. Use fertilizer that has been designed for acid-loving plants, and apply at half the normal rate. After the first year it is permissible to taper off, but the chances are you'll get better bud set and healthier plants by continuing to fertilize lightly.

Like conifers, rhododendrons and azaleas are generally disease-free and unaffected by pests and so need no regular spraying. The one pest to watch out for is the root weevil; the adults chew notches in the leaves, while the grubs feed on the roots. Petal blight is sometimes a problem. For advice on remedies, check with the local county extension agent.

With their shallow root systems, rhododendrons and azaleas are particularly vulnerable to droughts. Be sure to water periodically in the spring and early summer unless rainfall has been ample, and take pains to see that the soil does not dry out in late summer or early fall, for that is when the plants prepare themselves for the cold of winter. Finally, if autumn rain has been sparse give the roots a good soaking before the ground freezes in the late fall or early winter. Such precautions are especially advisable the first year. Young plants need careful attention the first twelve months so that they can adjust to the conditions in your garden. Even a dwarf that has been guaranteed hardy to your area should receive extra protection the first winter. Mulch it extra heavily, or surround it with a fence of burlap. One veteran gardener covers her new dwarf plants with overturned bushel baskets until the weather warms up.

Pruning is a matter of taste — the plants do not otherwise need it except for the removal of dead wood. Bear in mind that these plants set their flower buds in the summer for the next spring's bloom, so any pruning should be done in the first few weeks after the blossoms have gone by. In the case of rhododendrons especially, you may want to remove spent flower heads after blooming is over in order to keep the plant from putting extra strength into seed formation. (Evergreen azaleas are not so constituted.) Not all experts agree, however, on the necessity of such "deadheading." With most dwarf rhododendrons and azaleas, whether or not you remove spent blooms, the chances are you will get superb, renewed bloom next spring — and enjoy once again in microcosm a sense of the incredible prospect that so awed Captain Kingdon-Ward.

Plant List, Dwarf Rhododendrons and Azaleas

RHODODENDRONS

For moderate regions of the United States (like Pacific Northwest)

Purples	SPECIES:	*R. polycladum, R. calostrotum riparium, R. chameunum*
	HYBRIDS:	'Prostigiatum A.M.'
Reds	SPECIES:	*R. forrestii repens*
	HYBRIDS:	'Carmen'
Pinks	SPECIES:	*R. ferrugineum, R. pemakoense, R. hirsutum flore plenum, R. williamsianum*
	HYBRIDS:	'Ginny Gee', 'Pink Snowflakes', 'Rose Elf'
Yellows	SPECIES:	*R. lepidostylum, R. lepidotum (elaeagnoides)* (yellow form)
	HYBRIDS:	'Chikor', 'Curlew F.C.C.'
Whites	SPECIES:	*R. edgeworthii, R. moupinense, R. leucaspis*
	HYBRIDS:	'Ptarmigan F.C.C.', 'Snow Lady', 'Small Gem'
Others	SPECIES:	White-pink: *R. roxieanum oreonastes*
	HYBRIDS:	Light blue: 'Sapphire', 'Bluette'. Chartreuse-yellow: 'Shamrock'

(Note: Plants listed below for colder regions are also generally acceptable in moderate areas.)

For the Northeast and other colder regions (Note: "?" indicates hardiness doubtful)

Purples	SPECIES:	*R. fastigiatum, R. russatum, R. rupicola*
	HYBRIDS:	'Purple Gem', 'Ramapo'
Reds	SPECIES:	None
	HYBRIDS:	'Baden Baden', 'Small Wonder'
Pinks	SPECIES:	*R. racemosum*
	HYBRIDS:	'Arsen's Pink', 'Ginny Gee', 'Waltham'

'Gumpo Pink' and, in lower left, 'Gumpo White' are two popular Satsuki
azaleas from Japan which generally grow no higher than about one foot.
(Photo by Pamela Harper)

Yellows	SPECIES:	*R. keiskei* (dwarf forms such as 'Yaku Fairy', *cordifolia* and 'Compact Form'
	HYBRIDS:	'Patty Bee'
Whites	SPECIES:	*R. yakusimanum*
	HYBRIDS:	'Dora Amateis'
Others	SPECIES:	Lavender: *R. mucronulatum* dwarf
	HYBRIDS:	'Veesprite', 'Wigeon'

For moderate regions

Purples	SPECIES:	*R. sataense* (varies from orange to lavender)
Reds	SPECIES:	*R. oldhamii*
	HYBRIDS:	'Betty', 'Greta'
Pinks	SPECIES:	*R. kiusianum, R. macrosepalum*
	HYBRIDS:	'Eliza Scott', 'Gumpo Pink', 'Welmet'
Whites	HYBRIDS:	'Yuka' (Gumpo), 'Midori' (Gumpo)
Others	SPECIES:	Salmon-orange: *R. indicum* 'Balsaminiflorum'
	HYBRIDS:	Orange-red: 'Ama Gasa' (Satsuki). Scarlet-orange: 'Flame Creeper'

For colder regions

Purples (including lavender)	SPECIES:	*R. kiusianum, R. yedoense poukhanense*
	HYBRIDS:	'Mme. Mab Chalon' (Robin Hill), 'Munchkin'
Reds	SPECIES:	*R. nakaharai, R. kiusianum* (red form)
	HYBRIDS:	'Joseph Hill' (North Tisbury), 'Alexander' (North Tisbury)
Pinks	SPECIES:	*R. canadense, R. kiusianum*
	HYBRIDS:	'Pink Pancake', 'Itsi Gishi', 'Gwenda' (Robin Hill), 'Cecile'
Whites	SPECIES:	*R. kiusianum* (white form)
	HYBRIDS:	'Yuka' (North Tisbury), 'Gunrei', 'Gumpo White'
Others	HYBRIDS:	Scarlet-orange: 'Flame Creeper'. Salmon: 'Michael Hill' (North Tisbury). Salmon-orange: 'Kazan' ('Ruzikon')

4

Woody
Ornamentals

ALTHOUGH DWARF CONIFERS or rhododendrons may be the backbones of the small-scale garden — the distinctive elements around which plants of even lesser stature will be organized — there are many other woody ornamentals equally handsome that can be particularly appropriate for a given site. If the range of choice in some cases may be limited when compared to that available to the conifer or rhododendron collector, that is often because hybridizers have only recently become intrigued by such plants or because unusual species or varieties have not yet been discovered in the wild. Sometimes the reason is economic: some unusual plants are expensive to propagate or raise, and the conventional garden center finds it difficult to make money on them. So they have often been hard to find. A great many specialty nurseries, however, carry them or at least know where to locate them.

It is well to remember that until fairly recently the smaller forms of conventional plants, those that were the result of genetic mutations or other aberrations of nature, were generally rejected as uninteresting or even unworthy. That is now changing: gardeners today are asking for them. Then too, some kinds of woody plants with dwarf forms, although they might have been potentially very popular all along, have for one reason or another been difficult to propagate — cuttings would root only infrequently—so that even specialty nurseries could not stock them. But since the mid-1970s, as demand for small plants has increased and as new techniques such as tissue culture — once thought to be practicable only with herbaceous plants — have been refined and extended to woody plants, many of these delightful small ornamentals are being produced in some quantity. More still are on the way.

Most prominent among the plants now coming into garden centers in greater number are the mountain laurels. They are members of the genus *Kalmia,* named by the great Swedish botanical classifier Carl Linnaeus for his disciple Peter Kalm, who had found and described many of the species during a tour of northeast America in the 1740s. Laurels have long been admired especially for their exquisite small saucer-shaped blooms. "This is the broad-leaf evergreen par excellence," wrote the great plant collector Ernest Henry Wilson in the early years of this century. "A clump of restful green for eleven months of the year, then an unmatched wealth of loveliness, a myriad of blossoms artfully fashioned, burst into clouds of white and delicate pink."

But partly because of propagation problems little experimentation was done on laurels until a generation ago. At that time a Connecticut plant geneticist and horticulturist named Richard Jaynes resolved to try broadening the range of plants available to the public. Jaynes was especially interested in creating compact cultivars of *Kalmia latifolia,* the mountain laurel of the eastern United States, as it tends to become leggy in its natural form. But he was also looking into such other species as *K. microphylla,* western alpine laurel, and *K. polifolia,* bog laurel. In his hybridizing crosses he found especially good results coming from two *latifolia* variants, *K. l. fuscata,* which has a brownish-purple band within its corolla ("banded" laurels are much prized by kalmia devotees), and the rarer *K. l.* 'Myrtifolia', which is a true miniature. It happened that tissue culture came into its own just as Jaynes's work was coming to fruition. (And thanks to tissue culture, 'Myrtifolia' is itself available now in some specialty nurseries; growing little more than two feet high after ten years, it presents white blossoms in the spring that are almost the size of a normal laurel's blooms.)

In 1983 Jaynes, who at that time was at Connecticut's Agricultural Experiment Station in New Haven, introduced a number of new cultivars to the trade, among them 'Elf', a dwarf whose light pink buds open to reveal a profusion of flowers that are a fetching off-white. Now operating his own nursery in Hamden, Connecticut, he has several more promising cultivars in the works, one of them a cross of 'Myrtifolia' with *K. latifolia angustata,* the willow-leaved mountain laurel. He hopes in time to produce a range of miniature laurels with flower traits currently seen only in the larger plants. Future fanciers of small-scale laurels will be the luckier for the wait.

Mountain laurels as a group are hardier than rhododendrons and are found in the wild as far north as southern Canada. But a particular form will be hardy only in relation to the area where it (or its parents, if it is a cultivar) was grown. It is a good idea to find out from a nurseryman where

Forming a perfect low mound, the dwarf holly *Ilex crenata* 'Helleri' sets off an entranceway. Below it is the so-called Loddon lily, *Leucojum aestivum*, a spring-blooming bulb, and in the foreground a tiny dwarf spruce just putting out its new growth for the year. (Photo by Pamela Harper)

his plants came from. 'Elf' is certified by Jaynes to be hardy to Zone 5. A more critical concern is mountain laurel's occasional susceptibility to winter kill, the desiccating effect of cold winds and intense midwinter sunlight. Young plants in particular benefit from protection from the wind and the harshest sun (light shade is best); a protective spray can also be a good idea, provided that two coatings are applied. Kalmias prefer soil that is on the acid side, just like rhododendrons — both are members of the heath family, the Ericaceae. Soil should be well drained and highly organic. Follow the same planting precautions as with rhododendrons, and mulch well (preferably with an organic mulch) to protect the roots, which grow near the surface. Be sure plants go into the winter with their root areas well watered. A final tip: as with rhododendrons, you may want to remove spent flower heads to ensure good bloom the following year.

The hollies, members of the genus *Ilex,* are a different story. Popular since Roman times as holiday decorations because of their distinctive spiky leaves and their strong winter color — and thought to have religious significance accordingly (some believe "holly" is a form of "holy") — they were for the most part represented in United States gardens until fairly recently only by the American holly, *Ilex opaca.* Other species, such as the more elegant English holly, *Ilex aquifolium,* were deemed insufficiently hardy or were simply not well known to horticulturists. But after World War II, as native stands of *Ilex opaca* were seen to be disappearing because of over-exploitation, nurserymen began turning to other varieties. Among those that now began to be made available in large quantity was the Japanese holly, *Ilex crenata,* which has been a mainstay of gardens in Japan for centuries.

A densely branched tree, some of whose forms may grow to twenty feet, the evergreen *I. crenata* is genetically somewhat unstable and produces more than its share of dwarfs. Gardeners in Japan like it for its unobtrusive quality — with its black berries it is not a showy plant — and for the ease with which it can be pruned to a felicitous shape; some gardeners espalier it. Everyone likes the special texture provided by its small, lustrous leaves with their scalloped ("crenate") edges; the plant is also relatively trouble-free. One good dwarf form is *I. c.* 'Helleri', which forms a low, twiggy mound; another is *I. c.* 'Dwarf Pagoda', which grows only about an inch a year and rarely attains a height of more than half a dozen inches. *Ilex crenata* is America's best-selling dwarf holly.

Somewhat similar to *I. crenata* in producing black berries is the aptly named inkberry, or *Ilex glabra,* an evergreen that is native to the United States. While *crenata* is hardy to Zone 6, *glabra* is even tougher, thriving as far north as Zone 4. Both species prefer acid soil, but while *crenata* demands good drainage, *glabra,* which is native to swampy areas, can endure wet feet. Both prefer full sun but can stand some shade. Although many *Ilex glabras* become too large and are thus not true dwarfs, a reliable form is *I. g.* 'Compacta Tankard Strain', a low grower that fruits heavily. Gardeners who want a dwarf holly with red berries can investigate *Ilex rugosa,* known as rugose holly, a prostrate shrub only a foot or two in height. It prefers shade.

Remember that with all hollies the male and female flowers (which are tiny) are on separate plants, so that to produce berries it is generally necessary to have a male tree somewhere near the female. (If your neighbor has one, that's good enough.) Competent nursery personnel can usually advise as to which is which.

Cultivated and venerated in Japan even longer than the Japanese holly is the familiar Japanese maple, whose delicate beauty has been honored by romantic poets in its native country since at least the seventh century. The principal species, *Acer palmatum,* has a tendency to produce wide variations as it grows in the wild, and over the centuries hybridizers in Japan, working with these varieties and with other species, have produced more than two hundred fifty cultivars. Big or small, the tree is virtually a must for any self-respecting Japanese gardener, and while some forms can grow forty or fifty feet tall there are plenty of dwarfs to satisfy the small-scale gardener in crowded Japan — or in the United States.

Aside from the refined grace of their slender branches, the Japanese maples are of course most noted for their almost bewildering range of leaf color. The foliage can be a brilliant crimson in the spring, green in the summer and red or gold in the autumn — and there are endless variations on these changes. The slim, lacy or even threadlike leaves may be maroon, tangerine-red, green-red or variegated pink-green or white-green, to name just a few. Fall color may be yellow, orange, purplish or bronze instead of red. Skilled gardeners have found that they can enhance autumn color by withholding water just slightly as the fall season gets under way, causing the trees to become even more splendiferous. Such treatment is admittedly risky, however.

The dwarf forms, which offer almost the full range of leaf color, are often grouped under the term *Acer palmatum* 'Dissectum' (referring to their divided leaves), though the proliferation of cultivars has resulted in much confusion in terminology and many dwarfs are not considered 'Dissectum' types at all. A good many are available in specialty nurseries in the United States, among them *A. p.* 'Red Pygmy', whose bright red or maroon leaves may turn purplish in late summer, and *A. p.* 'Beni Komachi' ("little red girl"), whose crimson-colored spring foliage turns to greenish-red in later months, each leaf edged in crimson. 'Beni Komachi,' says Tom Dilatush, a New Jersey conifer specialist who also raises Japanese maples, "is just plain likeable."

Such gems are assuredly welcome in any small-scale garden. Some care, however, must be given to their placement. Dwarf maples with predominantly green foliage can take full sunlight, though they may be burned by late-afternoon summer sun and accordingly benefit from protection. Red varieties are better off in the shade, although paradoxically their color is richer if they get some strong sunlight for part of the day. Trees with variegated colors demand afternoon shade at least in warm climates to prevent burning. As to soil, Japanese maples are not demanding, and because their roots are close to the surface they will thrive even when planted in a shallow layer of soil over a rock stratum. Be sure to set them no deeper than the level at which they have been grown, and mulch them well to protect the roots from both summer heat and winter freezing.

Providing a completely different look to the garden are the brooms, most of them members of the genus *Cytisus* (although some members of the genus *Genista* are also called brooms). They are known for their spiny, small-leaved stems, which rise fountainlike from a low base and put out lovely yellow or white, but sometimes red or purple, small flowers in the spring-time. (Brooms, incidentally, are not named for the implements used for sweeping. What happened was the reverse, broom plants centuries ago being cut and tied together for that use, until any sweeping device came to be so designated.) Many brooms are tough and vigorous — they are sometimes used in median plantings along American superhighways. As garden plants they are to be recommended for creating a decorative spreading effect year round. Although all the brooms hardy in the north are deciduous, their green stems retain a vibrant look through the winter, almost giving the appearance of evergreens.

Many brooms are large plants: the yellow-flowering Scotch broom, *Cytisus scoparius,* which is native to western Europe but is naturalized in milder parts of the United States, can reach eight or nine feet in height, whereas the white-blooming Spanish broom, *C. multiflorus,* from the Iberian peninsula, may exceed ten feet. Some other species are more appropriate for the small-scale gardener. The deciduous *C. albus,* or Portuguese broom, usually grows no higher than one foot in cultivation; hardy at least to Zone 6, it presents white or yellowish-white flowers in the spring. Still more reduced in size is *C. decumbens,* prostrate broom, with its rich yellow blooms; it too should be hardy to Zone 6. And note *C. x kewensis,* a durable cream-flowering variety that grows parallel to the ground. Gardeners in more moderate zones might want to try the purple-flowered *C. purpureus,* a deciduous species from southeastern Europe, which typically attains twelve to eighteen inches.

Brooms differ from many of the other plants mentioned in this chapter in decidedly preferring sun; shade is not for them. And while soil on the acid side is best, it can be poor and dry — avoid giving them too much nourish-

One of the low-growing brooms, *Cytisus x kewensis,* bears cream-colored or yellow blossoms in the spring. (Photo by Pamela Harper)

OPPOSITE: A Kingsville dwarf box, *Buxus microphylla* 'Compacta' (foreground), marks a stepped pathway in the garden of Harold Epstein in Larchmont, New York. (Photo by Pamela Harper)

ment. The major consideration, however, is that they are deep-rooted and react badly to transplanting. Pick a good spot for them and then do not disturb.

Somewhat like the brooms in appearance, and perhaps better known to most American gardeners, are the cotoneasters with their small white or pink flowers, their opulent berries (generally red or black) and their flat, almost fishbonelike branching habit. Most cotoneasters are fairly low growers but some species are much more prostrate than others. *Cotoneaster adpressus,* from western China, rarely exceeds a foot in height, and its branches root wherever they touch moist soil; good cultivars of this red-berried plant include *C. a.* 'Compacta' and the especially minute *C. a.* 'Little Gem', both hardy to Zone 6. Another variety, *C. microphyllus congestus,* is distinctive for its twiggy and almost contorted look; with its downswept branches it forms a compact, rounded mound. Cotoneasters like full sun but will tolerate some shade, and they grow best in fairly dry soil.

Lilacs, known botanically as the genus *Syringa,* are of course widely cultivated for their lavish and highly fragrant purplish or white blossoms. Most

of the thirty-odd *Syringa* species grow to majestic proportions, but one is pleasingly small. It is *S. meyeri* 'Palabin', also sometimes called *S. palibiniana,* which in time will reach only about three feet. It is hardy at least to Zone 6.

Not strictly speaking a dwarf, as it is naturally a very low grower and has no larger form, but demanding inclusion in any survey of woody ornamentals favored for small gardens, is bearberry, *Arctostaphylos uva-ursi.* Known as kinnikinnick in some parts of the United States, it is a prostrate, creeping evergreen shrub that makes a delightful ground cover. Its springtime flowers, white or tinged pink and bell-shaped, are followed by bright red berries (inedible), and its small leaves turn bronze in the autumn. Preferring sandy soil and full sunlight, it is much used at the seashore or in rocky areas. One problem with bearberry is that most of its more ornamental forms, developed largely in the milder areas of the western United States, have not proved hardy in the Northeast. Recently, however, an Oregon couple named Peg and Ray Preg found a variety that they named *A. u.-u.* 'Big Bear' and that seemed commendably tough. They sent it to Long Island nurseryman Jim Cross, and it has turned out to be hardy at least to Zone 6. It is much to be recommended.

Bearberry comes under the heading of an "easy" plant: very little upkeep is needed once it is established, and it will thrive if given sandy, acid and perfectly drained soil. Quite the opposite must be said of the daphnes, attractive plants native to southern Europe and the temperate regions of Asia. Daphnes are particularly popular among some of the more ambitious rock gardeners, who like to rise to challenges and dote on the plants' small, fragrant blossoms. But daphnes are finicky and unpredictable as to soil and are all too well known for suddenly expiring after several years of apparent health. Small-scale gardeners endowed with unusual patience can try *Daphne cneorum,* an evergreen shrub sometimes called the garland flower, which is hardy to Zone 4. Its narrow leaves, up to an inch long, are shiny above but less so underneath, and its rosy pink blooms, which are highly fragrant, show up in May. It rarely grows more than a foot high. It too is one of those plants that does not respond well to transplanting. Baffled by daphnes' unpredictability, one expert has written, "It may well be that some kinds are naturally short-lived." But Jim Cross insists he has never lost one that was given perfect drainage.

Much less aggravating, and perfectly appropriate for all manner of gardening situations, are dwarf forms of such well-known plants as *Andromeda,* bog rosemary; *Hydrangea; Pieris japonica; Mahonia,* Oregon-grape; *Gaultheria,* wintergreen; and both *Forsythia* and *Cornus florida,* or dogwood. For details of these and other possibilities, see the list at the end of this chapter.

Such an array of ornamentals may end up making quite a good-size garden — which may then demand an edging or border. What better than that traditional edging shrub, boxwood? For it too has its dwarf forms. The classic box species is *Buxus sempervirens,* or English boxwood — the formal plantings in Williamsburg, Virginia, are its best advertisement. This in turn has a dwarf form, *B. s.* 'Suffruticosa', known as edging box. Under normal circumstances edging box will grow no higher than about three feet, and assiduous trimming can keep it at a convenient one-foot height. This may satisfy many small-scale practitioners, although a smaller boxwood does exist. It is *B. microphylla,* known as littleleaf boxwood; a spreading plant, it normally reaches a height of only one foot but a width of three. A good cultivar is *B. m. koreana* 'Wintergreen', but there are others, and any of them could be the makings of a truly midget hedge.

That a grass could wind up this discussion of woody ornamentals may seem strange, but bamboos are indeed grasses. They are also woody, to a degree, and the dwarf varieties can be highly attractive additions to the small-scale garden. The bamboos are an extensive tribe, comprising no fewer than forty-five genera within the grass family. Most are tropical plants, of course, but three of the genera are hardy, and of these, one, the *Sasa* group, furnishes some bona fide dwarfs, plants that grow no higher than eighteen inches to two feet. For any garden at all, bamboos can be a distinct plus. They offer an exotic and at the same time serene look, they make a compact clump or screen — and they are virtually free of any possible disease or pest disfigurement. *Sasa pygmaea,* the likeliest species, is the world's tiniest bamboo, with bright green canes that are purply toward their tips and five-inch leaves bright green on the top and a dull silver-green underneath.

There is only one trouble with bamboos. Many are extremely invasive, and the invasive group includes all the *Sasas,* indeed all the hardy species, which extend their domain with astonishing speed by means of tough underground rhizomes. *Sasa pygmaea,* writes one authority, "moves horizontally with a rapidity that equals the vertical vitality of other bamboo species." It is possible though potentially exhausting simply to cut or pull up the invading shoots as they appear. A more practical solution is to confine the roots with some kind of barrier. The bamboo can be planted in a container to be sunk in the garden — but the obligatory drainage hole will surely constitute a viable exit for the rhizomes. Better protection is afforded by a trench filled with concrete or stone. Experts recommend sinking it to a depth of at least eighteen inches. That may seem like overkill to some, but to the devoted bamboo aficionado there is no question that it's worth every cubic inch.

A Selection of Woody Ornamentals

(H or W = height or width after twelve to fifteen years. Z = lowest estimated hardiness zone.)

ACER PALMATUM (Japanese maple) — Widely cultivated in Japan, with many varieties and some two hundred fifty cultivars. Dwarf forms are sometimes included under the group heading *Acer palmatum* 'Dissectum'.

> *Acer palmatum* 'Red Pygmy'. Very slow-growing. Leaves red or red-maroon becoming purplish in late summer. H 2' *A. p.* 'Beni Komachi'. Slow-growing. New growth is bright crimson, older leaves greenish-red edged with crimson. H 2' Z5

ANDROMEDA (bog rosemary) — Low evergreen creeping shrubs native to North America, Europe and Asia. True andromedas are not to be confused with plants of the genus *Pieris*, which are sometimes called andromedas.

> *Andromeda glaucophylla.* Pink flowers. H 2' Z5

> *A. polifolia* 'Nana'. A favorite with rock gardeners. Pink flowers. H 10" Z5

> *A. p.* 'Grandiflora Compacta'. Similar to 'Nana' but with white flowers. H 10" Z6

ARCTOSTAPHYLOS UVA-URSI (bearberry, kinnikinnick) — Prostrate, creeping, evergreen shrub native to cool zones of North America, Europe and Asia; forms low mats of greenery. Flowers (May) white or tinged pink, berries (late summer) bright red.

> *Arctostaphylos uva-ursi* 'Big Bear'. A particularly ornamental variety for use in colder parts of the Northeast.

BERBERIS (barberry) — Evergreen or deciduous spiny shrubs with red berries.

> *Berberis thunbergi* 'Atropurpurea Nana'. Japanese barberry, with lustrous bronze-red leaves. H 18" Z5

BUXUS (boxwood, box) — The classic evergreen hedge or edging shrub, native to temperate zones the world over.

A young wintergreen, *Gaultheria procumbens*, puts out its bright red berries in the fall. This plant is only a couple of inches high; even in maturity the creeping *Gaultheria* rarely exceeds six or eight inches. (Photo by Harold E. Greer)

Buxus microphylla 'Compacta'. Kingsville dwarf box. Forms a flat mound or compact bush. Prefers shade. H 1' Z6

B. m. koreana 'Wintergreen'. Similar to 'Compacta' but much hardier, can take full sun. H 1' Z5

B. sempervirens 'Suffruticosa'. English edging box much used for lining flower beds and paths. H 2–3' (but can be kept lower by trimming) Z7

CORNUS FLORIDA (white flowering dogwood) — Handsome deciduous tree with red autumn foliage, native especially to eastern United States woodlands.

Cornus florida 'Pygmaea'. A true dwarf dogwood. H 3' Z5

COTONEASTER — Decorative evergreen or deciduous shrubs known for their arching stems and fishbonelike branching patterns, their white or pink flowers and their red or black berries. Most are native to China.

Cotoneaster adpressus. Low-growing, deciduous, with branching more rigid than that of most cotoneasters. *C. a.* 'Compacta' grows no higher than 1'; *C. a.* 'Little Gem' is even flatter, often just 6", and much slower growing. Z6

C. dammeri, bearberry cotoneaster. A prostrate grower, with white flowers in early June. H 1' Z6

C. d. 'Strieb's Findling'. A smaller-leaved, exceedingly prostrate form. H 8–12" Z6

C. microphyllus 'Cochleatus'. Bright green leaves on a prostrate, slow-growing plant. Flowers white, berries scarlet. H 1' Z6

CYTISUS (broom) — Mostly deciduous shrubs characterized by long, supple green stems, small leaves and arching habit. Native to Europe. Most produce white or yellow flowers in the spring. They prefer sun and can take poor soil.

Cytisus albus. Portuguese broom. Flowers white or yellowish-white. H 1' Z6

C. decumbens. Prostrate broom. Yellow-flowering. H 6"–1' Z6

C. x kewensis. Semiprostrate. Cream flowers. H 1' Z6

C. purpureus. Purple-flowered. H 1'–18" Z6

DAPHNE — Evergreen or deciduous shrubs native to Europe and Asia. Flowers small and very fragrant.

Daphne cneorum, rose daphne. Evergreen, with rosy-pink flowers in spring. *D. c.* 'Alba' is a white-flowering form of 'Pygmaea' whose growth is slow and whose habit is flat. H 6" Z5

FORSYTHIA — The familiar deciduous, yellow-blooming shrub.

Forsythia 'Arnold Dwarf'. Originated in 1941 at the Arnold Arboretum in Boston. Tiny moundlike plant used better as a ground cover than for its flowers, which are minor. Its creeping growth makes a dense carpet. H 3" Z5

F. viridissima 'Bronxensis'. Produced in 1939 by the New York Botanical Garden, it is a bit larger than 'Arnold' but blooms more satisfactorily. H 1'–2' Z6

GAULTHERIA (wintergreen, checkerberry) — Evergreen shrubs from the Americas and Asia.

Gaultheria procumbens, wintergreen. A matting creeper native to eastern United States and Canadian woodlands which puts out small, barrel-shaped waxy-white flowers in spring and then, in the fall, bright scarlet berries that are sought by deer, grouse and partridges. H 4–8" Z4

HYDRANGEA — Shrubs known for their showy flowers whose color is affected by the soil's acidity.

> *Hydrangea serrata.* An excellent dwarf from Japan. Flowers generally white or blue (with circle of white or pink). H 2–3' Z6

ILEX (holly) — A large genus of some four hundred species of evergreen and deciduous trees and shrubs found all over the world and admired for their lustrous, generally spiky or toothed leaves as well as their copious red or black berries.

> *Ilex crenata,* Japanese holly. A low-growing, twiggy evergreen bearing black berries. *I. c.* 'Helleri' forms a low mound. Even smaller are *I. c.* 'Dwarf Pagoda' and *I. c.* 'Piccolo'. H 6"–1' Z5

> *I. glabra* 'Compacta', compact inkberry. Evergreen, bearing profuse black berries in the fall. A good cultivar is *I. g.* 'Compacta Tankard Strain'. H 3' Z4

> *I. rugosa,* rugose holly. From Japan. A prostrate evergreen shrub bearing red berries in August and September. H 2' Z4

> *Ilex x* 'Rock Garden'. A very dwarf hybrid ideal for small rock gardens. H 6" Z6

KALMIA (laurel) — Evergreen shrubs native to North America and bearing cup- or saucer-shaped flowers, generally white or pink, in the springtime.

> *Kalmia latifolia* 'Myrtifolia'. Dwarf mountain laurel, with white flowers. A cultivar, 'Elf', bears nearly-white flowers. H 2' Z5

> *K. polifolia.* Bog laurel. Flowers rose-purple. H 2' Z5

MAHONIA (Oregon-grape) — Evergreen shrubs native to North and Central America and east Asia, and noted for their leathery leaves, their showy racemes of small yellow flowers and their blue-black berries (which somewhat resemble grapes).

> *Mahonia aquifolium* 'Compactum', compact Oregon-grape. H 18"–2' Z6

NANDINA DOMESTICA (nandina, Chinese sacred bamboo) — Deciduous shrub native to China.

> *Nandina domestica* 'Nana Purpurea', dwarf nandina. White blossoms in the spring. New leaves have a pinkish tinge, turning reddish-purple

Pink flowers denote an unusual variety of the dwarf mountain laurel, *Kalmia latifolia* 'Myrtifolia'. (Photo by Harold E. Greer)

in the fall. Bright red or purple berries in fall and winter. Full sun or shade. H 18–30″ Z7

N. d. 'Harbour Dwarf'. A very dense plant, deciduous in the north, evergreen elsewhere. H 18–24″ Z7

N. d. 'Wood's Dwarf'. Compact evergreen plant, foliage orange to scarlet in fall and winter. H 18–24″ Z8

PIERIS — Evergreen shrubs native to North America and east Asia and distinguished by their dark green, short-stalked leaves and their clusters of urn-shaped flowers.

Pieris japonica 'Pygmaea', pygmy Japanese andromeda. An early flowerer (mid-April). Needs protection especially from the winter sun. H 2–3′ Z6

P. japonica 'Bisbee Dwarf'. Very small Japanese andromeda, nonflowering. H 2–3′ Z6

SASA (bamboo genus) — A group of small bamboos characterized by long leaves on short stems.

Sasa pygmaea. Pygmy bamboo — one of the world's tiniest. Highly invasive. H 6–18″ Z6

SPIRAEA (spirea) — Deciduous shrubs noted mainly for their white, pink or red flowers in spring and early summer.

Spiraea japonica. Dwarf spirea. Two good cultivars are *S. j.* 'Alpina' and *S. j.* 'Little Princess', both with rose-pink flowers. H 1–2′ Z6

SYRINGA (lilac) — Deciduous shrubs native to Europe and the temperate regions of Asia, and favored for their voluminous clusters of white or lavender springtime blossoms.

Syringa meyeri 'Palabini' or *palibiniana*. Violet-purple blossoms. H 3′ Z5

5

Heaths and Heathers

THE MOST IMPRESSIVE THING about heaths and heathers, says Jim Cross, is that they offer fascinating color changes the year round. Although the changes are often subtle ones, there is nothing quite like them in the whole plant world. Cross, a highly respected wholesale nurseryman on Long Island who specializes in woody ornamentals, many of them dwarfs, grows heathers in the garden around his own house and delights in showing visitors how intriguing the low-growing plants can be.

"Look at all those different colors just in the foliage — there are several shades of green, some browns, even a yellow or two. And the colors change during the year. Going into the winter, 'Blazeaway' over there changes from gold to orange. Another plant will go to a deep rust, while others will become almost black — you wouldn't believe it. The flowers that arrive in the early summer — pink, red, white or purple — are wonderful too. See those nice lilac-pink flowers on 'Tib' there at the edge of the garden? Here it is June. Those flowers will still be on that plant at freeze time. Notice I didn't say frost — I said freeze, maybe mid-December. And if you grow the winter heath, *Erica carnea,* you'll get flowers in midwinter — perhaps January, certainly February. That's pretty hard to beat."

Given such impressive credentials, it's too bad, he says, that so many people say they can't grow heathers, even when they live in a region that is appropriate to the plants. "All they have to do," he protests, "is pay attention to some simple rules, which happen to be very important. Like giving heathers very acid soil and plenty of sunlight. The plants will reward you richly. They are awfully easy to take care of. Many of them are hardy to zone four. They make excellent ground covers, holding the soil well and keeping weeds out. I'm pretty enthusiastic about them." So are a multitude of other gardeners, many of whom have created complete heather gardens in which these plants are the main attraction, set off perhaps by a few dwarf conifers or small shrubs and perhaps a Japanese maple or two.

Like every other heather enthusiast, however, Jim Cross is quick to acknowledge that the areas in which these evergreen plants can be grown are somewhat limited. That's because they require a climate that is fairly moist and does not get too hot in the summer. In the United States this ideally means the Pacific Northwest and parts of northern California, and the Atlantic coast states from Maine down to Virginia. (Heathers also flourish in western Europe and the British Isles, and in Japan and New Zealand.) Regions subject to harsh, dry winter winds are very hard on them, as are those with soil that is alkaline or heavy; that means, sadly, most of the midsection of the United States as well as the South — although the North American Heather Society boasts members (surely adventurous) in such unlikely spots as Illinois, Missouri, and even Florida. Aside from such enterprising souls, most gardeners in the center of the country may be forced to forgo the pleasures of the "hardy heaths," as they are called. Those in the more humid sections of Florida and southern California have one consolation: they may be able to raise the so-called Cape heaths, related plants from South Africa that are in effect tropicals — and that will not be covered in this chapter.

The special conditions demanded by heathers derive, of course, from their natural habitat. They are creatures of cool, wet wastelands, the kind of windswept moors and heaths that are especially characteristic of Scotland and other parts of the British Isles. Such areas are not hospitable to very many kinds of vegetation, in fact to much life at all; the word "heathen," in fact, is believed by some to derive from a word that meant a kind of outcast who was forced to dwell in an unfriendly place like a heath. But heathers thrive in such surroundings. "They are wild things," says Cross, "perfectly attuned to their environment. For example, they grow with great success on islands in the North Sea that are drenched by salt spray, and their seedlings will also take hold in the tailings outside mines in England. What do such desolate places have to offer a plant? Well, there's excellent drainage, and plenty of moisture. But the soil isn't very fertile — if you can call it soil at all." Dorothy Metheny, who presides over a lovely heather garden in Seattle overlooking Puget Sound and who acts as secretary of the North American Heather Society, recalls hearing once from a fellow enthusiast in Dorset, England, who boasted that he had "the most infertile soil in Britain." His heathers were in fine shape.

Rugged, persistent, the plants have been used by highlanders and moor dwellers for centuries not only for grazing their sheep but for such disparate

Several kinds of heathers, *Calluna vulgaris,* present their blooms in summer in the garden of heather specialist Greta Waterman in Freeport, Maine. (Photo by Greta Waterman)

functions as stuffing mattresses, thatching roofs and brewing ale. In England there have been laws on the books governing the burning of heather since 1401. But not all heathers are alike, and moor dwellers have had strong feelings about which ones are better for certain purposes. The true heather, or *Calluna,* was for a long time referred to by the English as the "He heath," as it was deemed better for grazing sheep, deer and grouse, while the other principal genus, *Erica,* was derided as the "She heath."

Such unfortunate prejudices aside, gardeners too have learned that there are differences among heathers that affect which kind may be better for certain garden purposes. "Heather" is a generally accepted inclusive term that refers to two genera in the Ericaceae family. One genus is the true heather, or *Calluna,* which is familiarly known as Scotch heather, or ling. It has just one species, *Calluna vulgaris,* although that species has many varieties. Native to western Europe and the British Isles, the callunas are for the most part quite hardy, are noted for their flamboyant foliage, and come into bloom from June all the way to late autumn. The other genus, *Erica,* consists of hundreds of species, all of them referred to by horticulturists as heaths. They come mostly from the mountains of southeastern Europe. The great majority of ericas are the Cape heaths, which do not concern us in this book, but there are at least a dozen species that are hardy to one degree or another and are thus of interest to gardeners in temperate zones. The heaths' foliage is not as colorful as that of the heathers, but they have one tremendous advantage: they flower at various times during the year, and their most popular species, *Erica carnea,* is the heath that blooms in the winter.

To the untrained eye, callunas and ericas — heathers and heaths — look very much alike. The botanical differences are indeed minor, having to do with the shape of the flower (the calluna's calyx, which is deeply cleft, is the

Erica (heath)

Calluna (heather)

showy part of the bloom, while the erica's corolla, which is urn-shaped, is what you notice). But there is a handier way to tell the two apart. Look at the leaves. Most of the erica's leaves tend to stand out from the stem almost like pine needles, while those of the calluna are scalelike and overlapping, and lie along the stem.

Although callunas and ericas make up the majority of so-called heathers sold in garden centers and nurseries, two other genera in the Ericaceae family (familiarly known as the heath family) are often associated with them and are sometimes available from specialty nurseries. One is *Daboecia* (pronounced dabbo-EE-shiah), native to the western rim of Europe plus Ireland and the Azores; its predominant species is *Daboecia cantabrica*, known as the Irish heath (sometimes as St. Daboec's heath). Daboecias put out flowers in the summer that are similar to those of the heaths but somewhat larger; most are rose-purple, but those of one popular variety, *D. c.* 'Alba', are pure white. Much sought after by rock gardeners, daboecias are unfortunately not dependably hardy much below Zone 7.

The other related genus is the so-called spike-heath, *Bruckenthalia*, which comes from the mountains of eastern Europe and Asia Minor. *Bruckenthalia spiculifolia*, its sole species, grows only six to eight inches high and puts out lovely rose-pink bell-shaped flowers from June through August; it is, however, only slightly hardier than the daboecias. In Zone 7 it will probably survive, but in 6 it will almost certainly need heavy winter protection.

The hardiest of all the heathers are the callunas, and because of their amazingly varied foliage they are especially prized by aficionados. Although there is only the one species, nurserymen and heather devotees over the years have produced a wide range of cultivars and varieties to choose from. Most have come about as chance seedlings rather than as the result of controlled hybridizing. (Heathers occasionally produce witch's brooms, the growth abnormalities that are more generally associated with conifers.) Almost all the callunas are quite low: few rise above two feet and most are a foot to eighteen inches high. Among the all-time favorites are 'J. H. Hamilton', a compact ten-inch plant with dark green foliage and double fuchsia-pink flowers; 'Blazeaway', twelve to fifteen inches high with yellow-green foliage that changes to orange-red and with pale lavender blooms; 'Beoley Gold', whose golden-yellow foliage darkens in winter and whose flowers are white; 'Aurea', whose green springtime foliage changes to gold and whose flowers are a rich purple; and 'County Wicklow', with bright green foliage and shell-pink double flowers. Gardeners looking for especially low callunas can search out *Calluna vulgaris* 'Foxii Nana', which grows no higher than four or five inches. White callunas, incidentally, have long been deemed omens of luck and are called "lucky ling"; some nurseries in Britain grow whites for what they term the "luck market," and the plants are much sought after for use in bridal bouquets.

Many callunas possess an added feature that is delightfully attractive in the winter. The side of their foliage facing the sun will be a much stronger color than the opposite side; when you walk around the plants, they appear to change color as you move.

Much more varied in size than the callunas are the heaths — which after all do comprise many species. One species, the tree heath or *Erica arborea*, commonly attains twelve to fifteen feet; its roots are used to make brier pipes, the name deriving from the French *bruyère,* for heath. The heaths that are of relatively small stature are (in addition to the familiar *Erica carnea) E. tetralix* or cross-leaved heath, a denizen of peaty bogs, with light pink flowers in summer and fall; *E. vagans,* the Cornish heath, which offers purplish-pink flowers from July to November (but which may grow up to three feet); and *E. ciliaris,* the Dorset heath, which does not exceed one foot and has bright pink summertime flowers. *E. scoparia,* the besom heath ("besom" is an ancient word for a broom for cleaning), is a species that normally grows up to ten feet, but it has a dwarf variety, *E. s. pumila,* that collectors admire for its rich dark green foliage.

Because of its delightful winter-blooming feature, *Erica carnea* has been the object of a great deal of attention — which has resulted in many excellent cultivars. By far the best known is *E. c.* 'King George', with deep rose-pink flowers that in some favored locations may break out as early as December and last until April. Another is 'Springwood White', a spreader whose white blooms may show up in February. 'Ann Sparkes', again with rose-pink flowers, is special among the winter heaths in having foliage that changes, going from golden bronze in the spring to gold with bronze tips later on, while 'Vivellii', with its carmine-red flowers, turns its foliage from dark green to bronze and then almost to black in winter. All the *Erica carnea* cultivars grow six to nine inches high. A nice feature of all the ericas is that their flowers do not drop when they fade but instead stay on the stems and turn a lovely russet brown color.

The winter heaths also can be counted on as hardy at least to Zone 6. Another question is how much warmth they can take in the summer. Some heath species, notably *Erica erigena,* will endure considerable heat; however, *E. erigena* is not a low grower. For small-scale gardeners in the warmer parts of California, for example, a good plant to try is an *Erica* hybrid, *E. x darleyensis* — which is a cross between *E. carnea* and *E. erigena.* It grows no higher than about eighteen inches. A cultivar, 'Darley Dale', performs well under heat and moisture conditions like those appropriate to azaleas, and produces masses of pale pinkish-mauve flowers at the same general time as the other winter heaths.

Likely to flourish especially where sea breezes can bathe them with moisture and also moderate temperature swings, heaths and heathers provide attractive groupings in Greta Waterman's lawn on the Maine coast. (Photo by Greta Waterman)

For any of the heaths or heathers to perform satisfactorily, however, they must be sited with care. All demand sunlight, the callunas in particular requiring at least six hours of sun every day throughout the year. The ericas prefer sun but will tolerate light shade (especially if it is from deciduous trees, which will be bare while the *Erica carneas* are in bloom). Two other considerations are a good supply of moisture and, for the callunas at least, protection against the desiccating effect of dry winter winds. (*Erica carnea* is not so vulnerable in the winter.) In some parts of the United States a south-facing slope will accomplish these aims. But in the Pacific Northwest, for example the Puget Sound region, the wet maritime winds preclude desiccation and are highly beneficial, and thus a west-facing slope is ideal. In the Atlantic coast states, where rain tends to come from the northeast but the severest low-humidity winds blow from the west or northwest, a northeast-facing or east-facing slope might be good, if it gets ample sun.

"Often the location alone won't provide sufficient protection, though," says Jim Cross. "So you have to break the force of the wind with some kind of fence or hedge. You could, of course, just cover the plants in the winter — but then you'd miss out on their extraordinary foliage color. Every garden is different. In each case you'll want to balance out the sunlight, moisture and wind protection factors the best way you can." He adds a special point for the winter-blooming heaths. "Put them where people will be sure to notice them as the plants come into flower — next to a path or beside the driveway, for example."

Although many good garden centers in the Northwest and Northeast sell heathers, the best selection is likely to be offered — as with so many small-scale plants — by specialty nurseries. A few nurseries deal in heathers alone. For some names and addresses, see the Appendix. Specialty nurseries will almost surely provide healthy plants. If you are picking them out yourself, look for those that are compact but vigorous growers, with fresh-looking foliage.

In preparing the site for planting, bear in mind that heathers as a group need acid soil and that they must have excellent drainage. They will flourish in soil with a pH of 4.5 to 5, although some of the ericas are somewhat tolerant of more alkaline surroundings. To achieve a soil mix that remains acid over a long period of time and drains well, be sure to double-dig it (removing one layer of soil, turning over the layer beneath and then restoring the upper layer) and add to it plentiful amounts of humus or peat moss, or better yet both (it is difficult to have too much). To be on the safe side, many gardeners also construct raised beds for their heathers, building an entire soil bank of peat and humus on top of their regular soil and enclosing it with stones, bricks, planks or railroad ties. Such raised areas will also set off the plants well, avoiding the monotony that can occur when so many plants are the same height. Some heather devotees achieve the same effect by varying the level surface of the soil to create a wave effect of numerous hillocks, or by using species and cultivars of different heights.

Although with the proper precautions heathers may be planted almost any time during the year (even in winter, if the ground is not frozen), early autumn may be the optimum as it gives the roots time to adjust before the onset of winter. Early spring is virtually as good, however, and may be the time when you will prefer to buy your plants.

Set the plants into the soil deeply, with the lower foliage at the level of the earth. Plants should be separated from each other so that they will not eventually crowd each other out; a good rule of thumb is four plants per square yard, although some of the low-growing callunas can be closer together. After a few years they will have come together to form a dense mat, choking out all lower growth. In the meantime, to keep weeds out as well as to protect the delicate surface roots, apply a good organic mulch — pine bark, fir bark and pine needles are all good.

But apply no fertilizer: this is important, for as Jim Cross points out, "These are low-fertility plants." They will obtain all the nourishment they need just from the mulch. They will, however, need adequate watering when young. Just how much is a tricky question, particularly in the case of callunas. "You've got to wean them from the ample watering regimen they got in the nursery," says Cross. "So water them regularly for a bit, then cut back gradually. Callunas are actually very drought tolerant in the summer. The first year, as you are watering them on your reduced schedule, keep an eye on the tips of the branches. If they begin to curl over, like a button hook, that's a sign the plant needs water, and right now. Water immediately; the tips will straighten out. Going into the first winter, make sure their roots are wet. After that you can just about forget watering, except in a severe drought. Normal rainfall will take care of them just fine." In some West Coast areas, however, a bit more watering may be needed.

The only other maintenance chore is pruning — what might be called the annual crew cut, for callunas in particular. Give the callunas a good "butch" haircut every year in the spring; late March or early April is the best time, before the sap starts to flow. (The winter-blooming ericas can be cut back after their flowering, but only if they need it to be kept in bounds.) Shearing the callunas will remove most of the previous year's growth, open up the interior of the plants to light and air and generally invigorate them. Have no qualms: the plants will be the better for it and live longer. "If you walk on the moors of Scotland," says Jim Cross, "you'll find that for the most part the heather will be a light brown. But here and there you'll see bright green patches. Those will be places where sheep have been grazing, or where there has been a fire. Cutting back has made the plants healthier."

Sometimes heavy pruning can save a plant that seemed dead. If despite the best precautions a calluna has suffered badly from desiccation in the winter, it will enter the spring season totally brown. That plant, you will say, has had it. Not necessarily so, says Cross. At the appropriate time — the end of March at the latest — cut it back severely, all the way to green wood. "Cut until you can see a good green cambium layer," he instructs. "Get all the dead wood off it. Then cease worrying. Turn your back on it and ignore it. Chances are it will bloom on time and look great."

Some Heaths and Heathers to Try

BRUCKENTHALIA (spike-heath) — Members of the heath family (Ericaceae) that differ from true heaths *(Erica)* in minor aspects of the flower's construction.

> *Bruckenthalia spiculifolia,* spike-heath or Balkan heath. Low and compact, with deep pink flowers from June to August. H 6–9″ W 10″ Z7

CALLUNA (heather) — Known especially for their extraordinary foliage, but most varieties and cultivars also bloom attractively in the late spring, summer or fall.

> *Calluna vulgaris,* Scotch heather. The lone calluna species. The small-foliaged shrubs may be anywhere from six inches to three feet tall, but all the varieties and cultivars listed below are under eighteen inches.

Notable for unusual foliage:

C. v. 'Aurea'. Foliage changes from chartreuse to copper. Mauve flowers from August to October. H 12″ W 24″ Z6

C. v. 'Beoley Gold'. Golden-yellow foliage that deepens slightly in winter. White flowers in August and September. H 12–15″ W 24″ Z5

C. v. 'Blazeaway'. Yellow-green summer foliage changes to orange-red in winter. Pale lavender flowers in August and September. H 12–15″ W 24″ Z5

C. v. 'Silver Queen'. Silvery-brown foliage. Lavender flowers in August and September. H 12–18″ W 20″ Z5

C. v. 'Sister Anne'. A prostrate plant. Silvery foliage with a brown tinge, turning dull bronze in winter. Mauve flowers from July to September. H 2–4″ W 12″ Z5

Notable for flowers:

C. v. 'Foxii Nana'. Extreme dwarf with bright green foliage. Mauve flowers in August and September. H 4″ W 10″ Z5

C. v. 'J. H. Hamilton'. Dwarf with dark green foliage. Double pink flowers from August to October. H 6–9″ W 18″ Z5

C. v. 'Nana Compacta'. Dwarf with bright green foliage. Lavender flowers from July to September. H 6″ W 12″ Z5

C. v. 'Peter Sparkes'. Dark gray-green foliage. Rose-pink double flowers from August to October. H 15–18″ W 30″ Z5

C. v. 'Tib'. Dark green foliage. Deep lilac-pink double flowers from June to November or December. H 12–18″ W 15″ Z5

C. v. 'County Wicklow'. Bright green foliage. Shell-pink double flowers from July to September. H 9–12″ W 20″ Z5

DABOECIA (Irish heath) — Members of the heath family (Ericaceae) that differ from true heathers *(Calluna)* and heaths *(Erica)* in flower details.

Daboecia cantabrica, Irish heath or St. Dabeoc's heath. A natural bog plant ideal for rock gardens. *D. c.* 'Alba' bears white flowers from June to October, while *D. c.* 'Atropurpurea' has deep purple blooms over the same period. H 18–24″ W 24″ Z7

ERICA (heath) — A wide-ranging genus characterized by needlelike foliage. Many appropriate species exist, with blooming periods throughout the year.

Erica carnea, winter heath or spring heath. The best-known heath for North American gardeners, blooming as early as February in some areas, or even earlier depending on site and climate.

Notable cultivars:

E. c. 'Ann Sparkes'. Foliage golden-bronze in the spring, turning gold (with bronze tips) thereafter. Rose-pink flowers from February to May. H 6″ W 9–12″ Z6

E. c. 'King George'. Dark green foliage. Deep pink flowers may appear as early as December and last to March or April. H 9–12″ W 15″ Z6

E. c. 'Springwood White'. Light green foliage. White flowers from January or February until May. H 8″ W 24″ Z6

E. c. 'Vivellii'. Foliage dark green with a tinge of bronze. Flowers deep rose-pink from January or February until May. H 9″ W 15″ Z6

Erica x darleyensis. A hybrid of *Erica carnea* and *E. erigena* that can stand warmer temperatures than *E. carnea.* The best-known cultivar, 'Darley Dale', presents pale lilac-pink blooms from midwinter to May. H 15–18″ W 36″ Z6

E. ciliaris, Dorset heath. Foliage mid-green. Pink or white flowers appear in June and last until late fall. H 9–12″ W 15″ Z6.

E. scoparia 'Pumila', besom heath. A dwarf variety of a heath from the Mediterranean region, with glossy dark green foliage. Red-tinged, greenish flowers from late spring. H 18″ W 24″ Z7

E. tetralix, cross-leaved heath. A good plant to try in cool, slightly damp sites. Gray-green foliage with white undersides. Numerous cultivars are available, blooming from June through October. H 8–12″ W 15–20″ Z4

E. vagans, Cornish heath. Upright plants that may be too big for the small-scale garden; but some cultivars are slow-growing and attractive. Flowers white, pink or purple. H 18–30″ W 24–36″ Z6

6

Miniature Roses

O NE OF THE CLEAREST SIGNS that gardeners are turning increasingly to plants that are smaller or less time-consuming, or both, is the current boom in miniature roses. As recently as the 1960s the miniatures, sometimes called "fairy" or "baby" roses, were not taken very seriously. If they happened to be enjoying a sales spurt at any one time it was considered a passing fancy, a fad that would play itself out. In the 1970s it did not play itself out, and while sales of conventional, full-size roses have remained flat or have even sagged somewhat over the past decade, the minis are going strong.

A case in point is the story of Nor'East Miniature Roses, Inc., a young company that was founded in the late 1960s as a backyard hobby operation by a Gloucester, Massachusetts, businessman named Harmon Saville. A soft-spoken, wry, unassuming man whose broad twangy speech betrays his roots in the Bay State, Saville knew little about plants and had never raised roses of any kind until in 1966 one of his sons gave him some miniatures for Christmas. But soon he was hooked and he and his wife decided to start a mini-rose business as a hedge against their retirement years. Their list of customers grew and in 1973 Saville quit his job and moved the whole operation to Rowley, Massachusetts, north of Boston. If sales were going up it was certainly due in large part to Saville's imaginative creativity and singular promotional talents, but the expanding market was there and he rode it with great acumen. In the early 1980s he astonished his competitors by leapfrogging across the United States to start a West Coast branch in Ontario, California, whose climate is undeniably more friendly to commercial rose growing than that of Massachusetts. Nor'East is now the biggest grower of miniature roses in the United States, and the orders keep pouring in.

"The question everyone asks," says Saville, "is how long it's going to last. I think miniatures will keep on taking a larger piece of the market. Of course I'm prejudiced, but there are good reasons why it should happen. Miniatures, besides being extremely attractive, are easier to grow than big roses because, being small, they are more manageable. They can be grown in more constricted places than the big roses — on apartment balconies or in window boxes, for example, and even indoors under certain conditions. They are hardier than the big ones, so you can grow minis farther north — people who formerly could not grow roses now often can, and we have customers in both Nova Scotia and Alaska."

He might have added that many of the miniatures bloom for several months at a stretch, and benefit from being cut for arrangements. The variety of plants available commercially is furthermore expanding all the time as hybridizers introduce new strains. Where once only a few colors were on the market — white, red, pink and a few yellows — minis are now sold in every color seen in big roses, and there are miniature climbers, minis that grow well in baskets, and even miniature moss roses.

With popular success has also come official recognition. Long slighted by proper rosarians, miniatures are now given annual Awards of Excellence by the American Rose Society (Nor'East copped four out of the five given in one recent year) and have recently been admitted into the trials for the prestigious All-America Rose Selection, the industry's top honor.

Contrary to widespread assumption, miniature roses are not plants that have been artificially stunted or dwarfed. They are naturally, genetically small and take their place in the spectrum of roses alongside the hybrid teas and floribundas as separate, definable entities. By general agreement in the rose industry, a miniature must have a flower no larger than one and a half inches in diameter. Equally important, all other features of the plant must be, as Saville puts it, "typical of the variety" — that is, in proper proportion. "Leaves, stems, everything must be appropriate," he points out.

Fully grown bushes are anywhere from about six inches high to more than a foot; some may grow larger if given plenty of root room. Within the mini class is a subclass called micro-minis whose blooms are extra small — no bigger than three-fourths of an inch across. "The blossoms on 'Cinderella', for example," says Saville, "are only about half an inch wide. Its buds are the size of a grain of wheat." The smallest micro of all is 'Si', bred by the Spanish hybridizer Pedro Dot; its light pink flowers measure just a quarter of an inch across. Unfortunately, 'Si' is very difficult to find these days.

An assortment of miniature roses is grouped above some coins to emphasize their small size. (Photo by Gary Mottau)

Given such beguiling characteristics, it is not surprising that miniature roses tend to bear names that are unabashedly cutesy. Dyed-in-the-wool horticulturists indeed are likely to wince at such sobriquets as 'Cuddles' and 'Puppy Love', to cite two current favorites. Nowhere else in the entire world of small-scale plants, in fact, are such names so prevalent. The hybridizers defend the practice on commercial terms: it sells plants. And any gardener who is looking for plants that will perform handsomely can afford to ignore the labels and recognize the minis for their superior qualities, which cannot be denied.

The origins of miniature roses are obscure. Most rosarians believe that today's minis are all descended, one way or another, from plants cultivated in China, the earliest center of rose growing. No miniatures have ever been found growing in the wild; the supposition is that long ago some rose fancier in China found a tiny flower that had appeared through some kind of genetic mutation and carefully preserved the strain through propagation. In the seventeenth and eighteenth centuries European sea captains trading in

Miniature Rose: 12"–15"

Micro: 6"–8"

the East obtained some of the plants and brought them to the West, and there was a brief vogue for them around 1800. But then interest died down and they were to all intents and purposes forgotten.

Modern appreciation of minis dates from a chance discovery that has acquired the status of legend among growers of the plants. In 1917 a Swiss nurseryman named Henri Correvon heard from a friend, one Colonel Roulet, about an extraordinarily tiny rose bush he had seen growing on a chalet window ledge. "It was a minuscule shrub," Correvon remembered being told, "five centimeters high, bushy, and covered with small roses not exceeding one and a half centimeters broad (just like a sixpenny piece)." The plant was said to have grown in the same pot for a century and "bloomed from one end of the summer to the other." Some modern theorists have speculated that such miniatures might have been obtained by the Swiss from relatives in Italy or southern France, where many early roses brought in from China were growing; they liked them because the plants were cold hardy in frigid Switzerland. Whatever the origins, Correvon was highly interested and acquired some cuttings. He dubbed the "pygmy rosebush" *Rosa rouletti* after his friend and sold it all over Europe. Miniatures were back.

Correvon was not a hybridizer, but one of his customers, a Dutch nurseryman named Jan de Vink, was. In the 1930s he began crossing *Rosa rouletti* with other roses to produce other miniatures; the factors that control miniaturization proved to be dominant, so that a mini crossed with a larger plant would usually result in another mini. Jan de Vink's best hybrid, a plant he named 'Tom Thumb' and patented, was a brisk seller on the Continent and came to the attention of the American rose-growing firm of

Conard-Pyle, which introduced it to the United States in 1936. Most American miniatures thus trace their lineage back to Colonel Roulet's discovery, although a handful of other miniatures subsequently found in England have also been part of the breeding armamentarium.

As recently as the 1960s, Conard-Pyle and one other firm supplied most of the minis sold in the United States. The other grower was Ralph Moore, proprietor of the Sequoia Nurseries in Visalia, California, who became excited about the small plants soon after Conard-Pyle brought in 'Tom Thumb' and who for a long time was almost alone in hybridizing them in this country. Moore is indisputably the grand old man of miniature roses, with more than two hundred fifty varieties to his name. Conard-Pyle itself has no breeding program, being strictly an importer and wholesaler, but it has introduced a great many successful roses to the United States trade, the most illustrious being the full-sized 'Peace', which is the most famous rose of our time. 'Peace' was developed in the 1940s by Meilland Roses of France, and it was Meilland that also, much later, bred the most notable miniature of all, the orange-red 'Starina', recipient of the highest rating ever given by the American Rose Society. On a scale of 10, 'Starina' gets a 9.4, higher than any other rose of any size ('Peace' itself pulls down only a 9).

Because no miniatures are found in the wild and the history of interbreeding is so elusive, there is understandably no market for species miniatures — indeed there is a question as to whether any true mini species exists. All the plants sold are cultivars, the work mainly of perhaps not more than a couple of dozen hybridizers in the United States and abroad. Most of the breeders are professional growers who, like Harm Saville, hybridize on the side to keep new product coming along, and who make hundreds of crosses each year yielding thousands of seedlings. But a few amateurs operate with great success. One who has made his mark is Frank Benardella of New Jersey, a businessman who breeds roses for fun and who was at one time president of the A.R.S. Benardella recently achieved a color breakthrough with his 'Black Jade', an extremely dark red (almost black) miniature that Nor'East has introduced to the trade. Among the professionals working with miniatures, one of the most productive — in addition to Saville and Moore — is Nelson Jolly of Rosehill Farms in Galena, Maryland. Another is Ernest Williams of Dallas, Texas. Altogether, the hybridizers are likely to introduce as many as two dozen new cultivars each spring, and at any one time there will be perhaps eighty to one hundred on the market, with just a dozen or so accounting for the majority of the sales.

The foremost concern affecting any gardener's decision as to whether or not to try miniature roses (or any other roses, for that matter) has to do with sunlight. To bloom satisfactorily roses must have at least four hours of sun a day. Intermittent or dappled shade is allowable at certain times of the day, and may even be an asset during the midday hours, but the total of four must be obtained (five or six is much better) or there is no sense growing them. Gardeners who keep their minis in pots can always move them to follow the sun, and indoors the plants will do well on a south-facing windowsill or under lights; but miniatures planted in the garden must get that direct light. Other considerations are less vital. Soil should be on the acid side — a pH of 5.6 to 6.5 is best, though anything from 5.5 to 7 is permissible — and should be humusy, with good drainage; it must not get soggy. As Harm Saville has said, "Any soil that grows good weeds is okay for roses."

In choosing specific cultivars it's a good idea to figure out what effect will be desired. Some roses are known for their fragrance, others for their colorful blossoms. Many are scaled-down versions of the hybrid tea, with a high center and petals that curl back, while others look more like old-fashioned shrub roses with their multiplicity of small petals and rounded form; some "singles" put out just five simple petals. The climbers grow long stems that can be trained up a wall or trellis, and they also are favored for hanging baskets, or for trailing out the front of a window box. Overall it may be worth pondering the essential nature of the plants: they are lowland creatures, not alpines, and their brilliant colors may in some cases be at odds with the more muted effect given by upland plants like dwarf conifers or heathers. In a bed by themselves they present no such conflict. Just how to combine them with other plants is of course very much a matter of personal taste.

Many good garden centers offer a fair selection of miniature roses, but a far greater range is available from the specialty growers, like Nor'East and Sequoia (see Appendix). If you buy from a garden center, be sure to steer clear of plants that are suspiciously large and bushy even though labeled as minis: they are almost certainly cut-down floribundas and will eventually outgrow the small-scale garden — if indeed they survive at all. No such imitations are sold by the reputable miniature specialists.

Most minis are sold in small plastic pots, though a few nurseries ship them bare-rooted. If you are planting more than one, set them about twelve inches apart. If possible cultivate the soil thoroughly before setting the plants in. Potted plants should be set in a hole that is about twice as wide as the pot and almost twice as deep. Sprinkle bonemeal or superphosphate in the bottom of the hole and mix it with some of the soil, then set the plant in (making sure the roots are freed up from the root ball) and fill around the roots with soil; the plant should be set so that its own soil is covered by a quarter to half an inch of new soil. Bank the rest of the soil around it to provide a reservoir, then water it liberally. Bare-rooted plants (which must be set in the ground immediately upon arrival) need a larger hole; separate

In one of his greenhouses Harm Saville, proprietor of Nor'East Miniature Roses, picks a bouquet of his minis. (Photo by Gary Mottau)

the roots and work the soil around them to make sure there will be no air pockets. Do not tamp the soil down by foot — let the water do the job gently.

All roses need fertilizing, and minis are no exception. Any water-soluble balanced fertilizer will do the job. The first application should be at planting time; thereafter, you can apply as often as indicated on the label. Some mini growers recommend, however, that fertilizer be applied at half strength but twice as often for maximum results. A helping of fish emulsion once or twice a year can make the plants still healthier.

As with all other small-scale plants, a good mulch not only protects the roots against temperature extremes but conserves soil moisture. In the case of miniature roses it also prevents splattering of soil on the low-hanging blossoms and foliage. Any good organic mulch — bark chips, buckwheat hulls, cocoa bean hulls, pine needles, leaves or compost — will serve. Be sure to renew it as needed.

The key to watering miniature roses is to keep the soil moist but never soggy, and to keep it from drying out. If it is loam on the heavy side it may need watering only every week or ten days; sandier soil may require attention every two or three days, and more often still during hot, dry spells. When watering be sure the soil gets a thorough soaking down at least a foot, to reach the deepest roots.

A good pruning every spring keeps the plants compact and also promotes better blooming. Wait until leaves begin to appear, then cut plants back severely to two to four inches above the ground. At any time later in the year, if a plant seems to be getting too large, simply shear it off. It will thrive under such seemingly violent treatment.

Although the minis are hardy up to at least Zone 5 they do need protection during the winter in colder areas. In the fall their leaves change color and drop off as they prepare for their winter rest. Pile up leaves, evergreen boughs or salt hay around them, or cover them with an inverted wastebasket or plastic bucket. In more moderate areas (Zone 8 or warmer), no extra protection need be applied. In very warm regions, however, the gardener should force the plants into dormancy in January by pruning them severely and cutting back on water — but without letting the soil get completely dry.

The one remaining concern is protection against pests and diseases. Like all roses, the miniatures may be not only attacked by such bugs as spider mites and aphids but afflicted by black spot or mildew. But largely because they are so small, they are much easier to care for than their full-size counterparts. You can usually get rid of spider mites, whose presence shows up in the form of dull areas along the midribs of the leaves, by dousing the undersides of the leaves with a vigorous water spray every day; be sure to keep dousing for at least two weeks to break the egg-larva-egg cycle. The presence of tiny webs under the leaves indicates a heavy infestation; remove all the leaves and flush heavily with water — this should banish the mites and the leaves will soon grow back. If the mites nevertheless persist or other varmints appear and flushing does not work, use whatever spray is recommended by a good garden center, and be sure to follow the directions on the label precisely.

Black spot, that familiar bane of all rose growers, shows up in the form of black dots (with a halo around them) on a plant's lower leaves, which will have turned yellow. Mildew manifests itself as a whitish fuzzy growth under the buds and on tender new growth. Both can be banished by a good fungicide (garden centers all have them) sprayed at the dosage and interval specified on the label. If your own gardening experience indicates to you that such fungus ailments are likely because of local conditions, you might want to inaugurate a spraying program as soon as you acquire the plants. Or if you desire totally perfect, disease-free plants at all times, say for exhibition purposes, similar vigilance might be in order. But many gardeners find a more relaxed attitude is perfectly permissible: if disease has not struck, do not assume that it will. Just keep the plants trim and well washed, and treat with chemicals only if trouble occurs. Until it does, sit back and enjoy these amazing small bloomers.

Some Popular and Dependable Miniature Roses

'Acey Deucy' — Medium red tea-type with black overlay on reverse of petals. Hybridizer: Saville. H 12″

'Buttons 'N Bows' — Profuse pink to red blossoms. A good garden plant, the most widely grown pot miniature in Europe. Hybridizer: Olesen. H 12″

'Centerpiece' — Medium to dark red tea-type blooms on vigorous but compact plant. Hybridizer: Saville. H 14–16″

'Cupcake' — Compact, vigorous bush producing copious pink flowers. Hybridizer: Spies. H 11–14″

'Dreamglo' — A bicolor, with bright red and white flowers. Hybridizer: Williams. H 18–24″

'Green Ice' — Apricot-colored buds open into double white flowers that change to light green. Hybridizer: Moore. H 8″

'Heartland' — Coral-red flowers, a good plant for garden growing. Hybridizer: Saville. H 14–18″

'Holy Toledo' — Orange flowers with a yellow base, plant very vigorous. Hybridizer: Christensen. H 15–18″

'Julie Ann' — Vermilion-orange tea-type flowers appear through most of the season. Hybridizer: Saville. H 12–14″

'Lavender Jewel' — Lavender blossoms occasionally edged in magenta. Hybridizer: Moore. H 10″

'Magic Carrousel' — Red-and-white bicolor. Hybridizer: Moore. H 15–18″

'Pacesetter' — Nearly-white tea-type blossoms, very fragrant. Hybridizer: Schwartz. H 18–24″

'Peaches 'N Cream' — Peach-cream tea-type flowers. Hybridizer: Woolcock. H 15–18″

'Puppy Love' — Flowers are blend of orange, pink and yellow, always one per stem; good for cutting. Hybridizer: Schwartz. H 12–15″

Nor'East's 'Rainbow's End' won an Award of Excellence from the
American Rose Society in 1986. (Photo courtesy Nor'East Miniature
Roses, Inc.)

'**Red Flush**' — Profuse double light to medium red blooms on compact plant. Hybridizer: Schwartz. H 15–18″

'**Rise 'N Shine**' — Clear yellow flowers blooming almost continuously on vigorous bush. Hybridizer: Moore. H 15″

'**Simplex**' — A single, with just five petals, white with yellow stamens. Hybridizer: Moore. H 15–18″

'**Snow Bride**' — White blossoms with tinge of yellow inside. Hybridizer: Jolly. H 15–18″

'**Starina**' — Luminous orange-red blossoms with yellow base. The highest rated rose. Hybridizer: Meilland. H 14–18″

'**Winsome**' — Lilac-lavender double blooms. Hybridizer: Saville. H 15–20″

MICRO-MINIS

'**Cinderella**' — White flowers with a touch of pink. Hybridizer: de Vink. H 8–10″

'**Spice Drop**' — Salmon-pink flowers on a very compact plant. Hybridizer: Saville. H 6–8″

7

Miniature Bulbs

THE SIGHT, WHILE PREDICTABLE, is always a surprise: on a cold, blustery day in January or February a tiny but radiantly bright purple or yellow crocus will abruptly push up through the winter-hardened ground to reach for the sun. For gardeners of all stripes, the sight provokes potent feelings of expectation, for it means a new gardening year is officially under way, and spring will be along in just a handful of weeks. Even before the first crocus has appeared, in fact, there may have been other unlikely touches of color in the snowy scene to break winter's monotony — the demure but cheerful yellow-and-green blooms of winter aconites, perhaps, or a brace of snowdrops nodding white in the cold wind. Except for the winter heath with its sharp pinpoints of color (chapter 5), no plant or group of plants comes to flower so early as these in most United States gardens outside the subtropical regions.

It is no accident that the crocuses, aconites and snowdrops are all bulb plants, for bulbs are uniquely fitted to blossom at such unlikely times. It is furthermore no coincidence that they are also very small, for miniature bulbs are to a great extent creatures of the mountains, shaped and toughened by environmental forces to endure in the high country — but also capable of thriving in the average temperate garden. There are indeed a great many of these plants: the crocuses and snowdrops are just the beginning of a wide and rich selection of small bulbs — most no higher than six inches, but a few ranging perhaps up to a foot — that can keep the garden dotted with handsome swatches of color for a good part of the year. An enthusiast once noted that with luck the minibulb season begins in midsummer and continues through fall, winter and spring to end at the beginning of the following summer; some devotees maintain borders that consist of nothing but these tiny plants. Even in cold regions where continuous bloom is not achievable, miniature bulbs will extend the flowering season significantly at both ends.

Not only are the small bulbs welcome additions to the small-scale garden, fitting in well with dwarf conifers, rhododendrons and other plants of reduced stature. They are also, as all bulb admirers know, marvelously easy to plant and maintain. There are of course refinements that should be observed and will be spelled out below, but in essence it is only necessary to buy a bulb and pop it in the ground, and the plant will come up and keep doing its thing year after year, displaying its foliage, blooming gloriously, and finally dying back and disappearing, all right on schedule. Not unduly finicky about soil and hardly affected by any pests or diseases, bulbs are the closest thing to foolproof plants in the garden.

As with so many other small-scale plants, miniature bulbs have only in the past generation or so been appreciated by more than a few specialists. But their latter-day vogue has been more in the nature of a rediscovery than a brand new awareness. Some five hundred years ago, when bulb plants were first introduced to Europe by travelers returning from Asia Minor and points farther east, the smaller species were accepted as enthusiastically as the larger ones, for they were ideal additions to cottage gardens and to the compact "knot" gardens of European and British manor houses. With the coming of prosperous times to Europe in the sixteenth and seventeenth centuries, however, large estates surrounded by huge pretentious gardens became more and more the vogue, resulting in the cult of larger and more flamboyant plants, bulbs included, at the expense of smaller species. The trend was highlighted by the brief but spectacular "tulipomania" that swept Holland in the early seventeenth century and saw prized bulbs being traded for immense sums of money. That craze burned itself out — leaving in its wake the substantial Dutch bulb industry — but the larger bulb plants typified by opulent tulips and showy gladioli and lilies remained dominant until quite recently.

The principal clue to the popularity of all bulbs, including the miniatures, is of course that they are in effect horticultural storage devices that have adapted themselves to survive extended periods of drought or cold, or both, in their source regions. In areas like the mountains of Anatolia, for example, many months of subzero temperatures are succeeded by just two months or so of warm weather, during which time a plant must quickly flower, set seed and initiate buds for next year's growth. Bulb plants perform superbly under such stringencies, their flowers generating seeds and their foliage gathering nutrients that will be stored in the bulb during the long dormant period to come.

The exquisite pale lavender Tomasinian crocus, *C. tomasinianus,* makes
its appearance in January or February. (Photo by Pamela Harper)

OPPOSITE: A bed of grape hyacinths, *Muscari armeniacum,* is inspected
by a fledgling gardener. At the left are some full-size tulips. (Photo by
Gary Mottau)

Sometimes the dormancy will be characterized by severe drought rather
than cold; again the bulb survives underground, to put out new growth
when moisture and more benign conditions become once again available. In
many cases the underground storage unit is not a true bulb; tulips and
daffodils (and onions) arise from true bulbs, for example, while crocuses
and colchicums are produced from corms (which are usually a bit smaller),
anemones and winter aconites from tubers and irises from rhizomes. No
matter; the various devices function similarly, and all these plants are loosely
referred to as bulbs.

The great majority of miniature bulbs applicable to the small-scale garden
come from upland regions bordering the Mediterranean Sea or in the Balkans, Asia Minor or areas to the east. While such regions are far from arctic
in their winter temperatures, the high country can experience very low readings. So it is that most of the small bulbs to be considered here are certifiably
hardy: they will easily survive temperatures down to zero or minus 5 degrees, permitting gardeners as far north as Zone 6 to grow virtually all of
them and in Zone 5 to grow most. Some will flourish in Zones 3 or 4 (see

list on pages 101–106 for specific ratings). A large number of "tender" bulbs, many of them native to South Africa, can be grown in southern California and Florida and similar areas; but as they are not applicable to most temperate-zone United States gardens they will not be discussed here.

Because of the nature of their annual cycle, all bulb plants must undergo a dormant period; for spring-flowering bulbs, dormancy occurs from late summer to winter. Some bulbs, a good many crocuses for instance, need a hot and dry period in the summer, while others require moist conditions at that time. Spring-flowering bulbs generally need a period of cold during their dormancy; in warm areas like California it is often possible to chill bulbs in the refrigerator for a few months to satisfy this requirement.

Aside from these considerations — most of which will be satisfied automatically in the average garden — cultural requirements are simple. Most miniatures will grow in any good garden soil, but they prefer the mix to be just on the acid side of neutral, say between 6.2 and 7 pH. Soil with a pH below 6 or above 8 should be adjusted, by adding lime to increase alkalinity or sulfur to raise the acidity. The one important demand is for good drainage: in soggy soil most bulbs will rot (though a few actually thrive in wet surroundings). Some bulb enthusiasts create raised beds to ensure top-flight drainage, building up mounds of topsoil and enclosing them with planks, bricks or stones. A well-built rock garden will of course accomplish the same purpose.

Another concern is where the bulbs should be planted. Because in most cases they will remain buried for several years (being lifted only so that offshoots — new bulbs formed around the original — can be separated out) their surroundings must not be disturbed. Keep them away from garden areas that will be dug up often, as for example perennial beds where the plants may be divided every year or so. Planting under shrubs, on the other hand, is recommended as the soil is likely to be dried out in the summer by the shrub's roots, a condition favorable to many bulbs. A technique popular with many bulb growers is to naturalize them in rough grass or in a lawn, distributing them in random clumps as if they had grown there all by themselves. The small daffodils in particular look good when so disposed, as do crocuses, although bulbs that must be dry in the summer should not be planted in a lawn that will be watered at that time. Make sure, also, that the grass will not be mowed until the bulb's leaves have died back after flowering.

This in turn leads to the final dictum: never cut a bulb plant's leaves while they are still green, for removal of the foliage before it has fully ripened and turned yellow results in inadequate amounts of food being stored for the next season. The plant will put out smaller flowers or none at all, and will be severely weakened. Thus crocuses and other early bulbs may sometimes be planted in the average temperate-zone lawn as their leaves may have died back by the time the grass needs mowing; but note that even in the temperate zone many groomed lawns need their first mowing in late April, when crocus leaves are at their height. Later bloomers, like the species tulips which flower in April and May, are out of the question entirely for such treatment.

In any garden intensively planted with miniature bulbs the annual unfolding can be nothing short of glorious. In most years the first bulb to make its appearance — perhaps in late January or February, depending on the temperature zone — is likely to be the winter aconite, *Eranthis hyemalis,* whose buttercuplike yellow blooms rise on stems no higher than four inches to bring a delightful burst of color to the winter landscape. But snowdrops, *Galanthus nivalis* or *G. elwesii,* will be along almost simultaneously; *nivalis* is the easier of the two to establish, and a number of dependable cultivars of it exist (including a double form) that will be especially attractive to novice gardeners. Both *Eranthis* and *Galanthus,* like all spring-flowering bulbs, should be planted in October or earlier, as soon as they are received. Neither of them, incidentally, should be allowed to dry out before planting; *Eranthis* tubers should be soaked in water for a couple of days before planting.

Then come the crocuses: a large genus with some ninety species and numberless hybrids, whose cultivars can be obtained from most specialty nurseries and some garden centers. The species crocuses and their hybrids should not, incidentally, be confused with the widely sold large Dutch hybrid crocuses, whose blooms are two or three times larger; it is the species and their derivatives, less flamboyant but equally exquisite in their way, that are of particular interest to the small-scale gardener. Among the very early species are the golden crocus, *Crocus crysanthus,* with its bright yellow flowers, the yellow or orange *C. flavus* and the purple or whitish *C. imperati;* but the easiest of all to grow are the lavender or reddish-purple Tomasinian crocuses, *C. tomasinianus* — known as the "tommies." A few weeks later there will be additional species, most notably the Sieber crocus, *C. sieberi,* whose lavender or white petals bear a yellow throat. As to cultivars, *C. sieberi* 'Firefly' has lilac-pink petals and bright orange stamens — and there are many others just as intriguing.

A second wave of spring miniatures, in February or early March, may be ushered in by *Chionodoxa luciliae,* better known as glory-of-the-snow. It presents lilac-blue flowers with large white centers and yellow anthers on stems about six inches high; cultivars exist with pink or white blooms. Or the spring snowflake, *Leucojum vernum,* may offer its white flowers (tipped with green or yellow) on nine-inch stems.

The major performers at this juncture, however, are the early daffodils, members of the *Narcissus* genus. Two species stand out. The most unusual

America's native trout lily, *Erythronium americanum,* may bloom
anytime from late March to June. (Photo by Pamela Harper)

is *N. asturiensis* (also known as *N. minimus*) from high up in the Asturias
Mountains of northern Spain: a miniature yellow trumpet daffodil barely
four inches high, which the famed English garden authority Edward A.
Bowles once aptly dubbed the "neatest little gentleman in Europe." Better
known, if less bizarre, is *N. bulbocodium,* called the hoop petticoat daffodil
for its funnel-shaped golden-yellow tube with wrinkled margin. A third
species is *N. cyclamineus,* whose flowers resemble a cyclamen's in having
swept-back (or reflexed) outer petals; of *cyclamineus*'s many hybrids, an
especially fine choice would be 'Tête-à-Tête', which is only six inches high.
All the narcissus species naturalize well in grass or in a woodland setting.

As the weather warms and April commences, another cast of characters
moves in. Glory-of-the-snow's pale blue yields to the darker blue or purple
of the *Scilla* bulbs, known as squills, while alongside them appear *Anemone
blanda* or *A. apennina,* the windflowers from southeastern Europe and Turkey — daisylike blooms that may be deep blue, pink or red. Nearby also
may be *Erythronium dens-canis,* a European wildflower familiarly known
as the dogtooth violet (for its corm shaped like a dog's tooth); *dens-canis*'s
lilylike flowers are white to rose-colored. An American relative is the yellow-
flowering *Erythronium americanum,* whose mottled foliage is responsible
for its being called the trout lily. There will be the small, dark blue multiple

A planting of Siberian squill, *Scilla sibirica*, pokes its purple blossoms above a bed of pachysandra. (Photo by Pamela Harper)

blooms of *Muscari* (grape hyacinths). And as a center of attraction there will be the species tulips, graceful flowers averaging eight inches in height, far shorter and more restrained than the big hybrid tulips that have become such classics. The most popular of the species tulips are *Tulipa greigii*, with its scarlet to yellow blossoms, and *T. kaufmanniana* with its cream-colored flowers tinged with yellow or pink; both are originally from the southeastern reaches of the Soviet Union. *Greigii* can be identified by its foliage, which is streaked and spotted with chocolate brown; *kaufmanniana* is sometimes called the water-lily tulip as its flowers open flat in the sunlight.

Also making a show at this time will be the dwarf irises, in particular *Iris reticulata* and (somewhat later) *I. cristata* (crested iris), both with blue or violet flowers on four- to six-inch stems. Still later, into June, come the five-petaled, funnel-like blooms of *Oxalis laciniata,* which vary from pale blue to a deep mauve.

While no significant miniature bulbs bloom in early summer, the autumn-flowering species — of which there are several worth noting — should be planted at this time, and will have to be kept from drying out in the summer's heat. They begin blooming in most places in early September. One is a prominent member of the cyclamen genus (which also includes some spring-flowering species), *Cyclamen neapolitanum,* otherwise known as *C.*

hederifolium; its small butterflylike blossoms may be any color from rose to pink to pure white. Another impressive genus is *Colchicum,* sometimes (but erroneously) called the autumn crocus — though its flowers resemble the crocuses it is only a distant relative. (*Colchicum,* incidentally, yields an important and ancient remedy for gout.) A key miniature is *Colchicum autumnale,* whose rosy-lilac flowers appear unaccompanied by any foliage. (The foliage shows up luxuriantly the following spring and may be something of a problem; plant *autumnales* away from spring-blooming species to prevent the foliage from covering them.)

Finally there are the true autumn crocuses, blood brothers to the familiar spring varieties and fully as attractive. First to bloom may be *Crocus kotschyanus* (or *C. zonatus*), pale lilac or rosy-lavender, with a whitish or yellow throat. Another lavender is *C. speciosus,* whose petals bear dark purple veins. In some parts of the country the last of the autumn crocuses, or of the colchicums, may still be lighting up the garden in December or early January when the earliest spring species show up once again.

Confronted by such a parade of opportunities, many gardeners may wonder how to choose among them. Some of the specific information provided in the plant list on pages 101–106 may help to set guidelines. A good many of the species demand sun, while others tolerate shade or even prefer it. Some do best in dry soil, while others can tolerate much heavier, wet ground. The flow of colors, especially in the spring months, may point to certain choices: blues, purples and yellows abound in the miniature bulbs, and it may be a good idea to omit certain species or varieties so as to keep them from competing with each other. Yet the possibilities offered by contrasting colors, as between the bright blue of *Muscari* and daffodil's yellows, are also worth considering.

It is also possible, on the other hand, to extend the bloom time of a bulb planting by setting out some of them where they will get full sun and others where they will be shaded: the sunlit ones should be two or three weeks, at the very least, ahead of the others. Soil conditions can also affect time of bloom, bulbs in sandy soil flowering significantly ahead of those planted in a mix that is heavier in clay.

In most cases it is a good idea to set bulbs into the ground immediately upon receiving them. In the fall, however, spring-flowering species should be planted no more than six weeks before frost; crocuses should go in first but tulips can wait until the last minute. Most reputable bulb distributors will provide more specific instructions.

As many gardeners will recall, the rule of thumb on planting depth for bulbs is twice the top-to-bottom measurement of the bulb itself, but slightly deeper for small bulbs, corms and the like. In particularly cold areas, or in very light or sandy soil, slightly greater depth is advisable; and some miniature bulb devotees recommend greater depth in any case — about four inches for most, slightly less for the tiniest. As it happens, most small bulbs fortunately find their own depth in due course — if they are set too high, they somehow grow down to the correct level. If the bulbs are to be naturalized in a lawn it is easy merely to lift the sod, tuck the bulb or bulbs underneath and replace the turf.

In a garden bed, holes can be dug using a special bulb planting tool, although in many cases a trowel can do the job when the hole is relatively shallow. If a great many small bulbs are to be planted in a clump — and certainly a dozen or more crocuses or miniature daffodils can fit nicely into a single square foot of the garden — the best procedure is to dig a shallow trench the size of the clump, position the bulbs as desired and cover them. You may want to provide protection for such clumps. Gophers, mice, squirrels and chipmunks are fond of crocuses and tulips, though they ignore daffodils; narrow-mesh chicken wire buried around the bulbs should keep the marauders at bay.

Before placing each bulb in its hole or trench, be sure to add a dollop of bonemeal or low-nitrogen fertilizer to the soil immediately beneath it; wood ashes, which are high in phosphate, are also good. That should be the only fertilizing your miniatures will ever need; any extra nutrition they require in the future will be supplied by whatever mulch you provide for them. Any of the conventional mulches like fir bark or pine needles will do the job. If the bulbs are naturalized in a lawn or planted amid a ground cover like *Vinca minor* they will derive ample nutrients from the grass or other plants immediately above them.

Water the newly planted bulbs thoroughly right after setting them in, and make sure the soil around spring-flowering species does not dry out before winter sets in. Similarly, autumn bulbs should enjoy moist surroundings at least during the first summer. And you are likely to get better bloom if you water your bulbs periodically while they are in flower and immediately thereafter, until the foliage dies back.

Some purists recommend lifting bulbs each year after the foliage has disappeared, detaching any offshoots and replanting at the appropriate time. This may not be necessary in most cases, but if the clumps after a few years begin to get crowded and flowers become smaller, then by all means dig up the bulbs, separate any offshoots and start all over again. The display the following year should be better than ever.

Cyclamen neapolitanum is one of the dwarf bulbs that bloom in late summer or early fall. (Photo by John E. Elsley)

List of Miniature Bulbs

(H = Height of stem. Z = Hardiness rating. SP = Recommended spacing in a clump. SH = Tolerates shade.)

ALLIUM (flowering onion) — From Central Asia except as noted. Plants have round flower heads bearing multiple blossoms. All have odor of garlic when crushed (*allium* is Latin for garlic). All plants Z 3–4.

> *Allium acuminatum.* From Pacific Northwest and western Canada. Deep rose or lilac-pink blossoms in Apr.–May. H 6–10" SP 3" Must have sun
>
> *A. karataviense.* Silvery pink flowers in Apr.–May. H 6–8" SP 3"
>
> *A. moly,* golden garlic. From SW Europe. Bright yellow flowers in May. H 6–10" SP 3"
>
> *A. oreophilum.* Pinkish flowers in July–Aug. H 4–6" SP 3"

ANEMONE (windflower) — Spring-blooming plants from southern Europe or Turkey except as noted. All plants Z 4–8, and all SH.

> *Anemone apennina,* Apennine anemone. Light or dark blue daisylike flowers in Mar.–Apr. May not be hardy in Z4. H 6–9" SP 3"
>
> *A. blanda,* Grecian windflower. Deep blue, white or pink-to-red flowers in Mar.–Apr. H 3–6" SP 3" Prefers SH
>
> *A. nemorosa,* wood anemone. From England and European woodlands. Species is white, but cultivars may be lavender or blue. May flower anytime from Mar. to June. H 6" SP 3" Prefers SH

BRODIAEA — Late spring-blooming plants from the western United States bearing clusters of small funnel-shaped flowers.

> *Brodiaea laxa.* Deep blue flowers appear in June or July. The cultivar 'Queen Fabiola' is particularly popular. H 12" Z 6–10 SP 4"

CHIONODOXA (glory-of-the-snow) — Spring-blooming plants from Greece and the mountains of western Turkey.

> *Chionodoxa luciliae.* Star-shaped, light blue flowers with white centers (some varieties pink or white) in Feb. or Mar. H 6" Z 3–8 SP 3" SH

COLCHICUM — From the Alps and the mountains of the Balkans. Flowers appear in autumn except as noted. Resemble crocuses, but latter have whitish line down the center of the leaf while colchicums do not. Colchicums also put out their flowers before their leaves.

> *Colchicum agrippinum.* Pink-lilac flowers in Aug. or Sept. depending on the zone. H 4″ Z 5–9 SP 4″

> *C. autumnale.* Rosy-lilac flowers in Sept. or Oct. H 6–7″ Z 4–9 SP 6–8″ Prefers SH

CROCUS — Large genus of some ninety species, from the Mediterranean area and Asia Minor. All plants H 3–5″ and Z 3–7. SP 4″ for all. Where symbol M appears below, plants must be kept dry in summer.

> *Crocus biflorus,* Scotch crocus. White or blue flowers with purple veining, in Jan. to Mar. M

> *C. chrysanthus.* Yellow blooms in Feb. or Mar., but cultivars are available in other colors.

> *C. danfordiae.* Similar to *chrysanthus* but much smaller. M

> *C. flavus.* Bright yellow or orange blossoms in Jan. or Feb.

> *C. imperati.* Very early flowering: purple or whitish blooms with striped outer petals, in late Dec. in some zones, otherwise slightly later.

> *C. kotschyanus* (also known as *C. zonatus*). Pale lilac flowers with whitish or yellow throat, in Sept.

> *C. sieberi,* Sieber crocus. Lavender or white flowers with yellow throat, from Mar. and as late as June in some zones. Prefers M

> *C. speciosus,* showy crocus. Pale to deep lilac-blue flowers with veining of dark purple, in Sept.

> *C. tomasinianus,* Tomasinian crocus. Pale lavender to deep reddish-purple flowers, in Jan. or Feb.

CYCLAMEN — Tiny plants from the Mediterranean region with attractive foliage and bearing butterflylike blooms (with dark spot at mouth) at various times of the year depending on the species. All H 4–5″ and Z 5–9. SP 4–5″. All prefer SH.

> *Cyclamen coum.* Pink or magenta flowers from Feb. to May depending on the zone.

> *C. neapolitanum* (also known as *C. hederifolium*). White to deep carmine flowers in Sept. or Oct.

C. *purpurascens* (also known as *C. europaeum*), alpine violet. Rose-red flowers in Sept. or Oct. but perhaps earlier.

ERANTHIS (winter aconite) — Very early spring-blooming bulbs from Europe and Britain.

Eranthis hyemalis. Bright yellow buttercuplike flowers in Jan. to Mar. Needs moisture year round: soak tubers in water for several days before planting, and do not allow soil to dry out in summer. H 4″ Z 4–8 SP 3–4″

ERYTHRONIUM (dogtooth violet, trout lily) — Woodland plants native to Europe, Asia and North America. All Z 3–9 and prefer SH.

Erythronium americanum. Pale yellow flowers from late Mar. to June. H 8–9″ SP 5″

E. dens-canis. White to rose flowers from Apr. to June. H 6″ SP 4″

E. revolutum. Deep rose-pink flowers from Mar. to June. H 10–12″ SP 6″

E. tuolumnense. Yellow flowers with greenish center, Mar. to May. 'Pagoda' is a good cultivar. H 9–12″ SP 8–12″

FRITILLARIA (fritillary) — From Europe. Unusual flowers droop below the foliage.

Fritillaria meleagris, checkered lily or snake's head fritillary. Bronze, gray, purple or white flowers with checked pattern, from Mar. to May. H 6–12″ Z 3–8 SP 4″

F. pyrenaica. Deep purplish-brown flowers in Apr. to June. H 8–12″ Z 3–8 SP 4–6″ Prefers SH

GALANTHUS (snowdrop) — Very early plants from Europe and Asia. Both Z 3–8 and prefer SH.

Galanthus elwesii. Dainty white flowers in Jan. or Feb. H 6″ SP 3″

G. nivalis, common snowdrop. Small white flowers in Jan. or Feb. Many cultivars available, including doubles. H 4–6″ SP 3″

HYACINTHUS (hyacinth) — Fragrant spires of flowers from Europe and Asia Minor.

Hyacinthus amethystinus. White or blue flowers in May or June. H 4–10″ Z 4–10 SP 6″

IPHEION — Spring-flowering genus from South America.

Ipheion uniflorum, spring star flower. Pale to dark blue star-shaped flowers in springtime. The cultivar 'Wisley Blue' is highly recommended. H 6" Z 6–10 SP 4–6"

IRIS — Graceful plants from various parts of the Northern Hemisphere.

Iris cristata, crested iris. From eastern United States. White, light blue or lilac flowers with golden crests, in late spring. H 5–6" Z 5–10 SP 4–6" SH

I. reticulata. From Asia Minor. Pale to deep blue or violet flowers in Mar. or Apr. Many good cultivars available. H 6" Z 5–10 SP 4–6"

LAPEIROUSIA — Plants native to South Africa.

Lapeirousia laxa. Small star-shaped salmon-red flowers in the springtime. H 6–9" Z 7–10 SP 2–3"

LEUCOJUM (snowflake) — Plants resembling snowdrops but slightly larger, from Europe and British Isles.

Leucojum aestivum, the Loddon lily (from English river along whose banks it grows wild) or summer snowflake. Small white flowers with green markings, in Apr. H 12" Z 4–10 SP 2–4"

L. vernum, spring snowflake. White flowers tipped with green or yellow, in Feb. or Mar. H 6–9" Z 4–8 SP 4"

MUSCARI (grape hyacinth) — Plants from the Mediterranean area presenting clusters of dark blue or white flowers in spring.

Muscari azureum. Small blue or white flowers in Apr. or May. H 4–6" Z 3–8 SP 3" SH

M. botryoides. Blue blossoms in Apr.–May. A white form, 'Pearls of Spain', is also available. H 6" Z 3–8 SP 3" SH

NARCISSUS (daffodil) — Immensely popular genus from southern Europe and the Mediterranean area.

Narcissus asturiensis. Very dwarf yellow trumpet daffodil flowering in Feb. or Mar. H 4" Z 4–8 SP 2–3"

N. bulbocodium, hoop petticoat daffodil. Pale lemon-yellow to golden funnel-shaped flowers with fringed margin, from Jan. to Apr. H 6" Z 4–8 SP 4"

Iris cristata, or crested iris, displays its purple or white flowers in late spring. (Photo by John E. Elsley)

N. cyclamineus. Deep yellow flowers with reflexed outer petals, in Mar. Many good cultivars available. H 12″ (but cultivar 'Tête-à-Tête' is only 6″) Z 4–8 SP 4–6″

ORNITHOGALUM (star-of-Bethlehem) — Large genus of plants from Africa, Europe and Asia Minor.

Ornithogalum umbellatum. One-inch white flowers in the springtime. H 10–12″ Z 5–10 SP 8–10″

PUSCHKINIA (striped squill, Lebanon squill) — Squill-like flowers from Asia Minor.

Puschkinia scilloides. Pale blue flowers with blue-gray stripe on petals, in early spring. H 4–8″ Z 3–8 SP 3″ SH

SCILLA (squill) — Plants from southern Europe and Asia Minor bearing mainly blue or purple flowers (though some varieties white or pink) in spring. All plants H 6–10″, Z 4–8 and SP 3″.

Scilla bifolia. Pale violet to deep purple flowers in Feb. or Mar.

S. sibirica, Siberian squill. Purplish-blue flowers in Apr. A popular cultivar is 'Spring Beauty'.

S. tubergeniana (also known as *S. miczenkoana*). Pale blue or silvery flowers from Mar. to May.

TRILLIUM (wood lily, wake robin) — Spring-blooming wildflowers from the southeastern United States.

Trillium nivale, snow trillium. White three-petaled flowers in Mar. or Apr. H 4″ Z 4–8 SP 3–4″ Prefers SH

TULIPA (tulip) — Large genus from Asia Minor and the Soviet Union. The following are not to be confused with the large hybrid tulips that are better known.

Tulipa biflora. White flowers with yellow center in Apr. or May. H 8″ Z 4–8 SP 6″

T. clusiana, Clusius tulip. Flowers cherry-red on outside, creamy-white on inside, in Apr. H 8″ Z 4–8 SP 6″

T. greigii. Brilliant scarlet to yellow flowers with orange staining on outside, Apr. or May. Many cultivars available. H 8–12″ Z 4–8 SP 6″

T. kaufmanniana, water-lily tulip. Cream-colored flowers tinged with yellow and with pink on outside, Apr.–May. Many cultivars available. H 8″ Z 4–8 SP 6″

T. linifolia. Vermilion-red blooms in May. H 4″ Z 4–8 SP 3–4″

T. pulchella/violacea, red crocus tulip. Purplish flowers with black or yellow center; or reddish-violet, in Apr. H 4″ Z 4–8 SP 3–4″

T. tarda. White blossoms with central yellow eye, Apr. or May. One of the best miniatures, readily forms large clumps. H 4″ Z 4–8 SP 4–6″

ZEPHYRANTHES (zephyr lily) — Croeuslike plants from South America.

Zephyranthes candida. White flowers shading to green at base, in Sept. or Oct. H 5–8″ Z 7–10 SP 5–6″

8
Herbaceous Plants

W HILE THE SMALL-SCALE GARDEN may not lack for color during a good part of the year, especially in the spring when all
manner of bulbs are out and the rhododendrons and azaleas are
in full cry, there may be spells when very little is in bloom. Midsummer, for
example, is just such a time. Luckily, that is the height of the season for the
annuals, perennials and many other herbaceous plants, which can offer
stunning displays of color — and of intriguing shapes and textures as well
— from late spring right through to frost time. And as it happens there are
enough dwarf and miniature annuals, perennials, ferns and even ornamental
grasses available to satisfy the most demanding gardener who presides over
limited space. More varieties and cultivars are being introduced, too, all the
time.

Herbaceous plants — those that flourish during warm weather but die
back when cold arrives — can of course be an end in themselves, and many
serious gardeners grow nothing else. The familiar perennial border, surely a
glorious sight when well designed and meticulously maintained, is the most
notable result: a constantly evolving symphony of color throughout the
gardening season. A full-fledged, handsome perennial border, indeed, can
be achieved in miniature, as a glance at the list on pages 118–123 will
reveal. Yet it is hard to escape the notion that many small-scale gardeners
will be even more challenged by the opportunity to mix their herbaceous
plants with such others as woody ornamentals, heathers, bulbs and miniature roses, creating a garden that is uniquely satisfying all year long.

Many small herbaceous plants, to be sure, are not dwarfs or miniatures

Phloxes, alyssum and candytuft light up a border dominated by dwarf
perennials. (Photo by Gary Mottau)

OPPOSITE: Flowers of the prostrate *Phlox subulata* cover a rise of ground
in New England. (Photo by Gary Mottau)

at all; they just happen to be low growers. Most of the better-known ground covers, like *Vinca minor*, pachysandra and ground ivy, fall into this category — and will not be discussed here. The same holds true for herbs, the great majority of which can fit into most small gardens; they are a world unto themselves and should be studied separately for their own sake. Alpine plants, those tiny inhabitants of cold upland slopes which sometimes require a magnifying glass to inspect, are strictly speaking not dwarfs either, having no full-scale equivalent; but they are of great interest to rock gardeners and other small-scale plant specialists, and will be treated in the chapter following this one. What we are concerned with here are those plants that through genetic mutation or conscious hybridizing are scaled-down varieties of the familiar full-size garden plants. The only exceptions are the handful of well-known diminutive species, such as pansies and primroses, that in all honesty should not be ignored. But the range of scaled-down, dwarf herbaceous plants is considerable: there are dwarf varieties of astilbe, euphorbia, geranium, gypsophila, phlox, salvia and veronica, to cite just a few.

Given so many plants to choose from, even the most experienced hand may want to consider certain factors whose implications may serve to narrow the selection. For there is great diversity among all these plants, and no two gardens are alike (nor any two gardeners).

One factor is simplicity and convenience. In a garden patch already jammed with dwarf conifers, rhododendrons and heathers but in need of just a few spots of bright but continuous color here and there, the solution may be not perennial plants but annuals. Dwarf marigolds, impatiens or nasturtiums can be popped into a vacant spot at a moment's notice — and if one variety turns out to be not the right choice, another can be tried next year. Or if the vacant spot shifts because the garden is being rearranged, there is no deeply rooted perennial to disturb. One highly skilled small-scale gardener on Long Island has used annuals this way for years. "At the end of the season," he says, "I just let them go."

Another key consideration is scale. Most of the true dwarf herbaceous plants are less than a foot high — the average is six to eight inches — but a few range up to about eighteen inches. If a border consisted of nothing but six- to eight-inch plants it would be far from satisfactory; and so any choice of perennials for a mass effect will have to include some taller species as well as a few less than six inches high. Anyone planting the six-inch-high *Campanula garganica* for midsummer bloom, in other words, might want to plant some twelve- to fifteen-inch dwarf daylilies nearby. But if a garden area already consists of a number of larger plants like eighteen-inch dwarf rhododendrons or conifers, perennials that are of a uniformly smaller size might work well. The trick is to reduce all the relationships to a smaller

scale. Many species that are billed as "edging plants" under normal circumstances, like the moss pinks, *Phlox subulata* — suitable for placing along
the front edge of a full-scale border to face down larger plants — can become principals for the small-scale gardener, attracting attention in their
own right. But often a prostrate plant, or a thin spiky one, will be exactly
what is needed. For further thoughts on the design of small-scale gardens,
see chapter 12.

Local conditions will frequently determine what can be grown most successfully. Most perennials prefer soil that is just slightly on the acid side of
neutral; if your soil is markedly acid, for example because of the presence
of dwarf pines or junipers, no herbaceous plant that demands a more alkaline soil will be a good choice. Although most perennials benefit from full
sunlight, a few (hostas, for example) demand shade. Most, too, will do
better in soil that is kept fairly moist but is well drained, but some frankly
need dry surroundings. Where such details are relevant to the choice of a
plant they are mentioned in the list at the end of this chapter.

For many gardeners the key question has to do with succession of bloom.
Although many perennials bear handsome foliage that is admired for its
own sake, it is the flowering time and color that will in most cases determine
the choice, and most perennials bloom for no more than a few weeks.
Diligent perusal of the list (and of seed and nursery catalogues) can identify
a set of plants that will keep color unfolding throughout the gardening
year. In a sunny garden, for example, the display could get under way in
the spring with either the yellow-flowering *Alyssum montanum,* known
as mountain-gold, or the shrubby *Veronica prostrata* (or *rupestris*), which
bears bright blue flowers. Late spring and early summer could witness the
flowering of *Phlox stolonifera* (creeping phlox, with its blue, pink, white,
mauve or violet blooms), or *Dianthus deltoides* (a pink) with its pink or
white blossoms. As the summer progressed there could be the compact pink
blossoms of *Geranium dalmaticum,* or cranesbill geranium; or the daisylike
red blooms (with yellow tips) of *Gaillardia grandiflora* 'Baby Cole', a blanketflower cultivar. Finally in late summer and early fall the garden could
present one of the cultivars of the New York aster, *Aster novi-belgii,* which
is available in many colors, or one of the recently developed dwarf chrysan-
themums in yellow or white. All the forgoing plants can be counted on to
stay under seven or eight inches in height except for the New York aster,
which may grow to about twelve inches.

While a few of the dwarf varieties may be found at the better garden
centers — especially the marigolds, impatiens and other annuals — obtain-
ing the others may take some hunting. A few nurseries that specialize in
perennials may carry dwarfs; a few are listed in the Appendix. The best

The blanketflower, *Gaillardia grandiflora* 'Baby Cole', puts out red and yellow daisylike blossoms virtually all summer long and into fall. (Photo by John E. Elsley)

OPPOSITE: A container of dwarf marigolds accompanies other potted annuals and perennials on a terrace bordered with vertically trained *Impatiens*. (Photo by Gary Mottau, at the Victory Garden of station WGBH, Boston)

source is likely to be seeds. The catalogues of some of the major seed companies are worth exploring, for they are offering seeds for more and more miniatures and dwarfs all the time. But the widest selection will be found through seed exchanges like that maintained annually by the American Rock Garden Society. In addition to seeds for alpine plants the ARGS distributes seeds for everything from dwarf conifers to bulbs to heathers, and for the true devotee it makes the membership fee a real bargain. For the addresses of the ARGS and other plant societies, see the Appendix.

If you already have the kind of garden soil in which dwarf rhododendrons, bulbs and heathers thrive, you will find most perennials will do well in it: a light, humusy loam suits them fine, though they are tolerant of a wide variety of conditions. But if the garden is not so disposed, be sure to break up any hardpan and add copious helpings of peat moss, turning it thoroughly with a spade, fork or tiller; the main concern is to ensure adequate drainage, for few herbaceous plants survive soggy soil. Make sure (if necessary by sending a soil sample to the local county agent) that the pH rating is acceptable for the plants you envision, and correct accordingly. Just before planting, mix a well-balanced fertilizer into the soil.

As to the best time to get perennials into the ground, a good rule of thumb is to plant spring bloomers in the fall, summer and fall bloomers in the early spring. Small plants put into the ground in the fall, however, face a special problem: frost heaves during the winter may thrust them completely out of the ground. If in doubt, then, plant very small species in early spring. (Seed companies will provide advice with each packet on the best time to plant.) In general, give the plant as much time as possible to become accustomed to its surroundings before it is due to flower.

If the new plant is containerized, set it into the ground at the same depth it has been growing, and make sure it does not dry out either before or after planting; remember that plants need time to adjust to the open soil. If it comes bare-rooted, soak the roots in water before planting, and set it into the ground so that its roots are all thoroughly covered with soil. After firming the soil in place, water it well, and add a good organic mulch to a depth of around two inches. Keep the mulch away from the crown of any basal-rosette plant, however.

Assuming you have provided a good fertilizer before planting and an organic mulch afterward, no further feeding will be needed that year. It is a good idea, however, to renew the fertilizer each spring. The other key yearly maintenance chore, in colder parts of the country at least, is providing some kind of winter protection. Although virtually all the plants listed here are hardy to Zone 5 or 6, if not beyond, alternate freezing and thawing of the soil can hurt them. Covering the bed (or the spot where they are located) with evergreen boughs or salt hay during the coldest months, so as to minimize thawing, is a good precaution. Remove the protection as warmer weather returns.

As many gardeners are aware, perennials have a special need to be thinned out, via dividing, from time to time. Just when it will be advisable in the case of dwarf varieties will depend on the species and on your own gardening circumstances. If the plant appears crowded or congested, by all means divide it — early spring is the best time — by lifting the clump, prying the root structure apart and making two (or three or four) plants out of one.

It cannot be denied that herbaceous perennials may succumb to pests or diseases now and then. If you have planted many different species you will have helped minimize ailments, of course; on the other hand, a garden in which many plants are wedged in may suffer from poor air circulation. Slugs can afflict some perennials with special zeal; pick them off, or use the time-honored technique of setting out saucers of beer to trap them. Two big marauders of these plants are aphids and red spider mites. Minor infestations can often be controlled by vigorous spraying with water. If the attack proves serious, or if signs of disease such as leaf discoloration show up, consult your county agent for an appropriate remedy.

The dwarf ferns lend quite a different look to the small-scale garden from almost anything mentioned heretofore. Their delicate, lacy form may nevertheless be exactly what is needed in a certain spot. To anyone familiar with the well-known woodland ferns that seem to thrive only in shady, moist areas, some of the dwarfs are a revelation, as many are native to mountainous regions where they cling to cliffs and rock ledges and thrive under bright sunlight. The fern specialist Mareen Kruckeberg, who operates a rare-plant nursery in Seattle, has one species, *Polypodium hesperium,* that is only two inches high. That is its maximum height. Although it will never grow taller, however, it can be counted on to creep sideways.

Anyone contemplating ferns for the small-scale garden, then, should be aware that they are divided roughly into two groups (and are so classified in the list at the end of this chapter): the woodland ferns, which demand shade and a fairly high degree of moisture, and the mountain species, which can tolerate either sun or shade and which, while thriving under fairly wet conditions, must have superb drainage in order to survive. Both types need a humusy, porous soil mix — the ideal would be one that was heavily laced with leaf mold, or that even consisted entirely of it.

Any fern provided with good drainage but kept generally moist is likely to be free of pests and diseases. Occasionally they are prey to mealybugs or aphids. The best remedy in each case is a dousing of water to flush the visitors away. For the most part ferns need not be fertilized, though some gardeners give them a light feeding of fish emulsion once a year.

Yet another look to the garden — and one more akin to that provided by heathers and brooms — is offered by ornamental grasses. These too have their dwarf varieties. Admittedly it is difficult to get the same kind of effect from the lower grasses that can be obtained from the taller species, some of which may grow eight or ten feet high and sway alluringly in the wind. But any grass will provide a texture quite unlike anything else in the garden. Some of the dwarfs are hard to find; a few nurseries will carry them in containerized form and some of the large seed companies list them, but again a good source is one of the seed exchanges.

Grasses by and large are trouble- and maintenance-free, needing only an annual trimming to keep them in proper shape. In return they can reward the gardener hugely. Some do it with color: *Festuca ovina glauca* grows in the form of six- to eight-inch blue-gray tufts, while *Milium effusium aureum,* known as "Mr. Bowles's golden grass," is a brilliant yellow-green in the

Euphorbia myrsinites, spurge, yields entrancing chartreuse blooms in late spring or early summer. (Photo by John E. Elsley)

Asters are guaranteed to enliven any small-scale garden with their late-summer blooms. (Photo by Edsel Wood)

springtime, and some of the sedges, like *Carex morrowii expallida* (known as Japanese sedge), have cream-colored leaves edged in green. Others may provide motion: the fourteen-inch-high spikelets of little quaking grass, *Briza minor,* shiver and nod in a breeze. But perhaps the most delightful aspect appears in winter. Long after the annual flowers have disappeared and the perennials have retreated underground, the dry, golden stems and remnant plumes of the grasses remain, rising felicitously above a light snow covering to put on a show like no other.

Some Dwarf Herbaceous Plants

(SH: OK for shade.)

ANNUALS

Ageratum cultivars — 'Blue Danube', 'Little Blue Star', 'Blue Bedder'. Blue, lavender or pink blossoms. H 6–8″

Antirrhinum (snapdragon) dwarf varieties — Many colors. H 8–12″

Impatiens dwarf varieties — Pink, red, white or variegated. H 6″

Lobularia maritima (sweet alyssum) cultivars — Pink, purple or white. H 3–4″

Nasturtium dwarf varieties and cultivars — Scarlet, red, crimson or yellow flowers. H 6–9″

Nicotiana dwarf varieties — White, pink or red. H 12–18″

Petunia dwarf varieties and cultivars — Many colors available. H 5–7″

Tagetes (marigold) dwarf varieties — Yellow, red or orange flowers. H 5–6″

PERENNIALS

Achillea tomentosa (woolly yarrow) — Flat-topped yellow flower clusters from July to October. H 8–9″ Z 3–10

Alyssum montanum (mountain-gold) — Yellow flowers in spring on compact plants 6–8″ high. Z 3–10

Anemone pulsatilla (windflower) — Red, white or violet-blue flowers in April. H 6″ Z 3–9

Aquilegia flabellata 'Nana Alba' (dwarf columbine) — White 5-petaled flowers in mid- to late spring. H less than 1′. *A.f.* 'Mini Star' has blue-and-white flowers. H 6″ Z 3–9

Asperula odorata (sweet woodruff) — Often grown as a ground cover, but individual plants highly attractive. Tiny white flowers in late spring or early summer on compact plants 6–8″ high. Z 4–9 SH

Aster hybridus (Oregon aster) — Many cultivars available. Blue, white, pink or violet blossoms in late summer to early fall. H 9–15″ Z 4–9

Aster novi-belgii (New York aster, Michaelmas daisy) — Many cultivars available in various colors, blooming in late summer to early fall. H 6–12″ Z 4–9

Astilbe chinensis 'Pumila' — Mauve or pink flower spikes in late summer. Do not allow soil to dry out. H 8–12″ Z 4–8 SH

Aurinia saxatilis (basket-of-gold) — Small yellow flowers in spring. Plant must have good drainage. H 6–12″ Z 3–10

Campanula varieties and cultivars — Bell-shaped white or blue flowers from early to late fall. H 6–12″ Z 4–10 SH

Chrysanthemum cultivars — E.g. 'White Buttons', 'Yellow Buttons'. Flat, daisylike white or yellow flowers in late summer to early fall. H 6–8″ Z 4–10

Dianthus deltoides (pink) — Pink or white flowers on matlike bright green plants, in late spring. Prefers light, sandy soil. H 4–6″ Z 3–7

Euphorbia myrsinites (spurge) — Chartreuse flowers in late spring or early summer, on handsome plants with grayish foliage. H 6″ Z 5–9 SH

Gaillardia grandiflora 'Baby Cole' (blanketflower) — Daisylike red flowers with yellow tips, from early summer to late fall. H 6″ Z 3–10

Geranium dalmaticum (cranesbill geranium) — One-inch-wide pink flowers over dark foliage throughout the summer. H 6″ Z 4–8 SH

Geranium sanguineum prostratum (prostrate blood-red cranesbill geranium) — Magenta or pink flowers on moundlike plants all summer long. H 4–6″ Z 4–8

Gypsophila repens (creeping gypsophila) — Myriad white (or pink, in cultivars) blossoms on trailing plants throughout the summer. Must have soil on alkaline side. Plants taprooted, should not be moved. H 6″ Z 4–9

Hemerocallis minor (dwarf daylily) — Many cultivars available; yellow flowers succeed each other throughout the summer. H 12–15″ Z 3–10 SH

Hosta venusta (dwarf hosta) — Mauve flowers on 6-inch spikes rising above 3–4″ plants in late spring. Z 3–9 Must have SH

Iberis sempervirens (evergreen candytuft) — Dwarf hybrids 6–7″ high. White flowers cover compact plants in spring. Z 3–10 SH

Myosotis rupiola (alpine forget-me-not) (also called *M. alpestris*) — Light blue flowers with yellow center, early spring to early summer. H 6″ Z 3–10 SH

Phlox divaricata (Canada phlox) — Blue or white flowers in late spring. *P. d. laphamii* is a dependable variety. H 12″ Z 4–9 SH

Phlox drummondii — Rose, crimson, scarlet, yellow or white flowers in late spring. Often sold as an annual. H 4–6″ Z 4–9 SH

OPPOSITE·

TOP: Basket-of-gold, *Aurinia saxatilis*, blossoms copiously in the spring. (Photo by Pamela Harper)

BOTTOM: The matlike *Dianthus deltoides*, which rarely exceeds six inches in height, erupts in pink or white blossoms in the late spring. (Photo by Pamela Harper)

The diminutive maidenhair spleenwort, *Asplenium trichomanes,* thrives in nooks and crannies of stone walls and is hardy to Zone 3. (Photo by Pamela Harper)

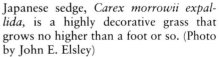

Japanese sedge, *Carex morrowii expallida,* is a highly decorative grass that grows no higher than a foot or so. (Photo by John E. Elsley)

Phlox stolonifera (creeping phlox) — Similar to *P. divaricata* but makes dense, creeping mats. Blue, pink, mauve, violet or white flowers in late spring. H 6–9″ Z 4–9 SH

Phlox subulata (moss phlox, moss pink) — Cultivars available in many colors. Prostrate. H 4–6″ Z 3–9 SH

Primula acaulis (English woodland primrose) — Creamy-yellow flowers in spring. Plants must be kept moist, but with good drainage; summer heat is hard on them. H 6″ Z 5–9 Prefers SH

Salvia varieties and cultivars — Scarlet or purple spikes of flowers in summer. H 6–9″ Z 5–10

Sedum (stonecrop) species and varieties — Clumps of starry flowers in spring, summer or fall depending on the species. H 2–18″ Z 3–10

Veronica fruticulosa — Short spikes of pink flowers in spring. H 6–12″ Z 4–9

Veronica prostrata (or *rupestris*) — Bright blue flowers on trailing, matlike plants in spring. Must have good drainage. H 6″ Z 3–9

Viola odorata (sweet violet) — Many cultivars available. Pink, white or purple flowers in late spring. H 8″ Z 6–10 SH

Viola tricolor (pansy) — Many cultivars available, in many colors. Blossoms appear from early spring through summer, but summer heat may hurt them. H 7–8″ Z 3–10 SH

FERNS — WOODLAND

Adiantum pedatum subpumilum (dwarf maidenhair) — Delicate circular fronds, with roundish leaflets, growing parallel to the ground. Fronds die back after frost. H 7–8″ Z 3–8

Asplenium platyneuron (ebony spleenwort) — Slender, tapering fronds with alternately spaced, tapering leaflets. Evergreen. H 6–12″ Z 3–8

Asplenium trichomanes (maidenhair spleenwort) — Slender fronds bearing rounded leaflets paired along dark stalks. Leaflets drop off after frost. H 6″ Z 3–8

Cysopteris fragilis (fragile bladder fern) — Thin, deeply cut feathery fronds. Deciduous. H 10″ Z 3–8

Woodsia ilvensis (rusty woodsia) — Lacy fronds smooth on top but bearing brown hairs and scales underneath. Deciduous north of Zone 6, evergreen from Zone 6 south. H 3–6″

Aspidotis densa (Indian's dream) (also called *Pellaea densa*) — Three-inch fronds, with pointed leaflets, on brown stalks. Spreads to form clumps. Evergreen from Zone 6 south. H 5″ Z 3–8

Camptosorus rhizophyllus (walking fern) — Long, thin spear-shaped fronds whose tips may take root. Grows well in rocks and crevices. Evergreen. H 4–12″ Z 3–8

Ceterach officinarum (scale fern) — Leathery fronds with round-tipped leaflets. Evergreen. H 1–2″ Z 3–8

Cheilanthes gracillima (lace fern) — Very thin, dainty fronds with hairy covering on undersides. Grows well on cliffs and ledges. Evergreen. H 2–4″ Z 3–8

Cheilanthes lanosa (hairy lip fern) — Similar to *C. gracillima* but with yellow-green or blue-green fronds. H 6–8″ Z 3–8

Pellaea atropurpurea (purple cliff-brake) — Narrow, widely spaced leaflets on purple stalks. Thrives on stone walls or dry ledges. Rare, endangered species which should not be collected in the wild. Evergreen. H 12–18″ Z 3–8

Pellaea brachyptera (Sierra cliff-brake) — Needlelike leaflets growing in clusters along knotted stem. Evergreen from Zone 6 south. May be difficult to grow in an open garden. H 16″ Z 3–8

Polypodium hesperium — Tiny fern with diminutive, leathery fronds. Only 2″ high, but will creep. Evergreen. Z 3–8

Polystichum kruckebergii — Another minuscule species, from the Olympic Mountains. H 2″ in cultivation, though it grows higher in the mountains. Z 7–10

Polystichum lemmonii — Similar to *P. kruckebergii* but 5–6″ high.

ORNAMENTAL GRASSES

Briza minor (little quaking grass) — 12″ high
Carex glauca (blue sedge) — 6″
Carex morrowii expallida (Japanese sedge) — 12″
Eriophorum latifolium (cotton grass) — 12–24″
Festuca ovina glauca (blue-gray fescue) — 6–8″
Milium effusium aureum (Mr. Bowles's golden grass) — 9–12″

9

Alpines

O NE OF THE LARGEST and most intriguing categories of plants
available to the proprietor of a small garden is made up of the
alpines. A great many experienced and enthusiastic gardeners, in
fact, concentrate solely on these denizens of the mountains. Any meeting of
the American Rock Garden Society, for example, whose members tend to
specialize in alpines, is likely to be dominated by tried-and-true horticulturists who seem almost to live in a separate world known only to them and
their friends, a world that may appear to be made up entirely of tough but
exquisite little plants barely a few inches high. One reason alpines excite
such devotion is that they represent several challenges wrapped into one:
many are difficult to find (garden centers and nurseries rarely carry more
than a few), some almost defy cultivation outside their native habitat, and
may require carefully contrived conditions in order to thrive in the garden.

But for their admirers the effort is certainly worth it. Alpines evoke a
mountaintop realm of sun, snow and bracing winds that many people consider exciting if not downright romantic. The very existence of the out-
wardly fragile plants under such arduous circumstances stirs wonder; the
fact that they can adapt to backyard surroundings is astonishing. And not
only are alpines enormously varied as a group, but their annual blooming
— after so many months during which they hardly change — can be spectacular. In the words of one of the leading experts on alpines, the Connecticut horticulturist H. Lincoln Foster, the plants "create moments of
excruciating pleasure."

Despite their reputation for difficulty, however, a large proportion of

---

OPPOSITE: Alpines and other rock plants line a pathway through the
Victor Reiter garden in San Francisco. (Photo by Pamela Harper)

alpines are not really hard to grow providing a few basic rules are followed. So while they are not to be classed as dwarfs or miniatures like most of the small-scale plants discussed in this volume (heaths and heathers, in chapter 5, make up the other exception), they can become a significant part of anyone's small garden and are therefore well worth knowing about. And as their apologists often remark, once you get into alpines it can be hard to stop.

The lofty terrain they come from, lying predominantly above the tree line, is anything but uniform: it can be rocky pastureland, cliffs or crags, assemblages of rocks known as screes or moraines, or even open meadow. When the plants are in their brief period of bloom (usually in late spring or early summer), observers are likely to be awestruck. The writer Ann Zwinger, who has hiked extensively in the upland domain all over the United States, gave a hint of the effect in her book *Land Above the Trees:* "It is easy to ignore the outside world and become totally immersed in a medieval tapestry of detail, each inch giving up a tiny treasure: a lapis lazuli gentian thumbtall atop a green silk thread; a lichen curled like starched lace . . . a small onion that offers its flowers like a bunch of lavender tulips . . . an alpine meadowrue with amethyst-rimmed leaves; a birdfoot buttercup pinched out of a pat of butter . . . a campion striped purple like a candy stick; an alpine oat grass with spun-glass florets. . . ."

Two things are responsible for the survival in the wild of most of these extraordinary plants: rocks and snow. Rocks provide shelter against murderous winds as well as a cool root run in the heat of summer, when the plants must flower; snow assures a protective blanket in the winter and a copious supply of water when the plants need it. Alpines often seem to be growing just from the rocks, without benefit of soil, but there is always soil somewhere, perhaps several feet down, which the roots can reach for sustenance — a plant two or three inches high may have roots three or four feet long nourishing it. The snow, in addition to shielding the plants from the onslaughts of the bitterest cold, often keeps them from renewing their growth until all danger of frost has passed in late spring. Their diminutive stature is not only an adaptation to the rigorous conditions (many take the form of tight cushions, or "buns," and their leaves are usually tiny) but a reflection of the short growing season each year, sometimes as short as six weeks to two months — there is not much time to add any height. But while the plants are very small their flowers are almost normally sized and thus seem even larger in proportion.

Because alpine plants habitually grow — and are grown by gardeners — among rocks or in soil with a high mineral content, there is an understandable confusion between the terms "alpine" and "rock garden." Briefly, a rock garden is a location, while an alpine is a kind of plant that can grow there — but so can many others, like sedums. A "rock garden plant," by general horticultural agreement, is anything that stays in scale and seems appropriate in a rock garden setting; the term includes not only alpines but mountain plants from below the tree line, like dwarf rhododendrons or miniature bulbs, and plants that just happen to be of small stature, like dwarf conifers (brought about mostly through genetic mutation) or heathers (natives of areas where the soil is poor). Rock garden plants that are not alpines tend to be far less demanding of their conditions, and some have very different needs — rhododendrons have shallow root systems requiring an organic mulch, for example, while alpines are deep-rooted and do best with a mulch of small stones that will keep their crowns dry.

Alpines thus occupy a special niche in the world of rock gardens, one that (like mountain air) is somewhat rarefied and, in the opinion of their enthusiasts, rather elevated. It goes way back: the first rock gardens in Europe were built sometime in the sixteenth or seventeenth century, mainly for growing mountain plants. The cultivation of alpines has always been considered a noble and esthetic calling. The painter Albrecht Dürer, who turned out a masterful canvas of a primrose as early as about 1500, was only one of a number of artists who found the plants of the higher reaches tantalizing.

But while alpines are generally associated with mountaintops, the scene is complicated by the fact that many genera are found at two or more elevations: some species of a genus will be alpine while others come from down the mountainside, even from woodlands. Primulas (primroses) are an example, some inhabiting boggy woodlands while others flourish in windswept alpine meadows. Phloxes are similarly diverse, as are gentians. In each case the alpine species are sun-loving and deep-rooted while the others tolerate or even prefer shade and moist surroundings.

Even the prototypical alpine genus of them all, the saxifrages — the name means "rock-breaker," referring to the roots' ability to reach down through clefts and crevices — contains species of both kinds. The more than three hundred species are broken down into groups that demand slightly different environments: the "encrusted" saxifrages, whose rosettes of leaves bear white encrustations of lime, prefer a slightly alkaline soil and protection from only the hottest summer sun, whereas the kabschia group is likely to prefer light shade throughout the growing season, and the mossy saxifrages, as their name suggests, must have a cool site and soil much richer than that required by the others. Other saxifrages are woodland plants and some grow along stream banks. Some prefer acid soil. Because they are so diverse, the saxifrages are among the most popular of all alpines, and they have been hybridized to an extent rare in this species-oriented garden group.

If rocks and wintertime snow are two standbys in the wild, one requirement above all is needed for the health of alpines in the garden: perfect

The delicate leaves of *Campanula garganica* provide an elegant backdrop for its purple flowers. (Photo by Pamela Harper)

drainage. Good drainage is beneficial to almost all the plants discussed in this volume; gardeners growing alpines have to learn to make almost a fetish of it. Water, applied frequently (emulating the melting snowbanks), must drain away quickly — thus the proliferation of rocks both above and within the soil. Almost as important is air movement: bred for the windy slopes, alpines abhor stagnation. Thus they often do better on sloping or even vertical surfaces, like stone retaining walls, than on level ground. A third basic need for most is protection from summer baking — which might seem surprising in view of their native diet of strong sunlight. But sun in the mountains is accompanied by cool temperatures (especially at night) and low humidity. As you cannot lower the humidity in areas of the United States like the hot Northeast or Midwest, the only answer is to provide shade, either by siting the garden on a north-facing slope or in the shadow of high-branched trees to the south, or by erecting some kind of lath device.

In view of these needs, combining alpines with other plants in a normal garden setting may seem difficult, for whatever benefits alpines may impede

A clay saucer serves as a tabletop rock garden for a group of pink
kabschia saxifrages. (Photo by Pamela Harper)

companion species. To some extent the drainage and soil requirements can
be localized, soil mixed so that it is more humusy in one area and less so
nearby. But many gardeners feel that creating a separate alpine setting
makes sense, and they point out that the small stature of the plants makes
this entirely feasible even in a small backyard — a perfectly credible garden
of alpines can occupy space only a couple of feet square, or can be planted
in the interstices of a stone wall that otherwise would be unused.

Constructing an appropriate home for alpines can be quite a task if done
properly, and there are many styles to choose from depending on what
particular kind of mountain environment is to be emulated. The minigarden
can suggest an alpine meadow, a scree (an accumulation of rocks of various
sizes at the base of a cliff or steep slope), a moraine (rocks deposited in an
area by glaciers or moving water, with water still moving through or under
it), a mountain stream or an alpine cliff face, to name just the most commonly attempted. Anyone contemplating such elaborate simulations is advised to obtain one of the many excellent books on rock garden con-

struction. Suffice it to say here that most of the styles contain the same elements. The basic soil has a high mineral content (small stones, gravel, grit) and is set up to provide a slope; large rocks are set into it tilting backwards so as to carry rainwater back into the ground rather than allowing it to run off; and the surface is mulched with stone chips to keep the plant crowns well drained and to forestall rot. Many rock gardeners satisfy these requirements by building a raised bed, the soil heaped up and held by flat rocks set around the edge like a small stone wall. Alpines can grow not only in the bed itself but in the retaining wall, their roots reaching into the soil for sustenance.

Two special kinds of alpine gardens, on the other hand, may be appropriate under certain circumstances. If your space is unusually limited or you wish to grow only a small number of alpines, the answer can be a trough garden, an adaptation of the old English practice of using an old sink or watering trough for a miniature plant display. A discussion of such troughs, which are generally made of concrete and bring together collections of small plants in the manner of modified bonsai groupings, will be found in chapter 13.

The other kind of specialized environment is an alpine house, a response to the special needs of certain plants. It is a kind of cool greenhouse whose

Set rocks into a slope tilted backwards so that they will lead rainwater back into the ground rather than allowing it to run down the slope.

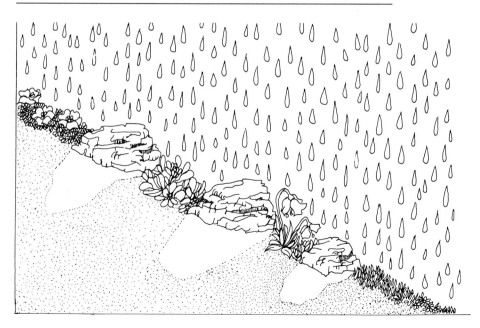

temperature in winter is merely kept from dropping below 32 degrees. During the cold months it maximizes the effect of the sunlight while keeping plants dry that must remain so, while in the summertime it can provide shade while remaining open to the breezes. It is possible to create a modified alpine house by adapting a cold frame or by constructing a special cover over a raised bed, but in any guise this is a contraption for the advanced amateur, one who has tried the easy plants and is ready for the really demanding ones. Users of such houses like to keep their alpines in pots so they can be readily moved as seems fit.

Good selections of alpine plants can, alas, be difficult to find, for despite the increasing interest in them in the United States few garden centers or nurseries sell more than a handful, if any. One excellent source on the East Coast is the Oliver Nurseries of Fairfield, Connecticut, which offers a great many species and also provides expert advice on growing them — but which unfortunately does not ship plants. A few other specialty nurseries may have alpine or rock garden departments as a sideline. On the West Coast the premier retailer is the Siskiyou Rare Plant Nursery of Medford, Oregon (see Appendix for details), which does ship. But dedicated rock gardeners all recommend joining a local chapter of the American Rock Garden Society (see Appendix), whose members habitually keep tabs on nurseries that may stock the plants, and which operates a seed exchange that is ultimately the best source for the more recondite varieties.

To any gardener accustomed to providing a soil that is rich and loamy, the leanness of proper alpine plant soil seems almost unreal. In sum, it consists largely of gritty substances with a touch of loam or leaf mold thrown in. Such, however, is what the plants are used to on those upper mountain reaches — they are conditioned to an environment in which they must struggle for existence — and it assuredly makes for superb drainage. The Oliver Nurseries recommends a mix of one part granite grit, one and a half parts gritty sand, a half part peat moss, one part leaf mold or compost and (finally) one part good garden soil. Anything richer will cause the plants to become weak and flabby and lose their look of tight efficiency. It may even cause them to grow unduly. "You have to provide the right conditions," says Oliver's alpine specialist, Priscilla Galpin, "so that your plant does not, as we say in the trade, turn into a horse."

Most alpines prefer a soil that has a neutral pH, although many do well with something on the alkaline side. There are no good rules of thumb governing the preferences of various kinds of plants; the best recourse is to check with whoever sells or gives you the plant or seed, though if in doubt keep the soil neutral. A handy way to provide the proper reading in the soil is to choose the kind of grit accordingly: limestone grit will push a mini-environment toward alkalinity while crushed granite will make it more acid.

Yellow-flowering *Sedum kamtschaticum* lines a quiet rock garden pool.
(Photo by Pamela Harper)

Often a single rock will suffice: a granite rock dug in next to an acid-loving plant will supply it with runoff water on the acid side, while a chunk of tufa — volcanic rock that happens to be limey — if buried underneath a plant needing lime will imbue the roots with just what they need.

One virtue of having plants that are of very small stature is that their placement is of minor consequence: none is likely to grow up to shade another or mar the overall effect. The one consideration to bear in mind is the tendency of some alpines to spread with some rapidity. Potential spreaders should be given enough elbow room at the outset to forestall later crowding.

If placement is not important, the actual planting is. Because most alpines are deep-rooted, it is essential to dig a deep enough hole to receive the roots adequately. Water the plant before setting it in, and add more water when you have refilled the hole around it halfway up. Set the plant high enough so that a mulch of at least an inch of pebbles can be added atop the soil, and firm the soil solidly — Lincoln Foster declares that doing so with your foot is not excessive. Then add the pebbly or gritty mulch. Throughout the alpine garden the mulch should be at least an inch thick; two is better. A light dressing of fish-emulsion fertilizer may help start a newly planted alpine on its way, but be sparing — the plants are not used to heavy feedings.

Alpines are largely maintenance-free. During droughts they may need some watering, but it's a good idea to proceed only if their leaves seem to wilt, and to apply water only on cool, windy days if possible. Pull any weeds that come up through the mulch the first year (there should not be many if the mulch is thick); thereafter, you may want to wait until the suspected invader comes to flower, to make sure it is not a seedling of another alpine — many of which seed themselves readily — and yank it out only if it fails that test. Cover plants with pine boughs or similar light shading during the first winter — if your winters are especially cold, without predictable snow cover, a layer of salt hay or of spoiled hay from farmlands (if available) is a good additional precaution. In the spring of each succeeding year remove any winter protection before growth has started, top dress the garden soil with fresh (gritty) mix and renew the mulch.

As alpines are in fact mountain wildflowers and a great many varieties flourish atop United States ranges (especially in the Rockies and the ranges of the Far West), it may be tempting to try collecting plants in the wild. True, many alpines grow in profusion, and in their case at least no harm may be done. Yet a large number of alpines have been declared endangered species; furthermore, tramping indiscriminately across alpine meadows away from marked trails can do great damage, and alpine environments recover much more slowly from such abuse than those down the mountain. It is a good idea to check with your state's environmental agency before embarking on any expedition. The plants are so extraordinarily beautiful in their own domain, it would be too bad to hurt them in any way.

Some Popular Alpine Plants

(All plants prefer full sun and a very well-drained, somewhat gritty soil with a neutral pH, and are hardy to Zone 3 or 4, unless otherwise specified. H = Height while flowering.)

AETHIONEMA (Persian candytuft) — Dwarf shrubs from the Middle East that bloom in late spring.

> *Aethionema* 'Warley Rose'. Deep pink flowers on a compact cushion with steely blue or blue-green needles. Hardy only to Zone 6. H 3–10″

ANDROSACE (rock jasmine) — Tufted plants from the European Alps, spring-blooming.

> *Androsace sarmentosa.* Mat-forming plant that bears deep pink flowers on short stems. Prefers slightly acid soil. H 4″

> *A. sempervivoides.* Similar to *sarmentosa* but flowers are brighter, with shorter stems.

ANEMONE (windflower) — Plants mostly from Europe and the Middle East; some are bulbs (see chapter 7) but those listed here are fibrous-rooted. They bloom in the spring.

> *Anemone baldensis.* From the European Alps; blue-backed white blossoms up to 2″ across. H 6–8″

> *A. magellanica.* From South America; creamy-yellow or reddish blossoms. Prefers humusy soil. H 6″

AQUILEGIA (columbine) — A large genus generally preferring rocky settings like stone walls or screes, and blooming in late spring or early summer.

> *Aquilegia akitensis.* From Japan; blue and white blossoms. H 6″

> *A. discolor.* From Spain; blue blossoms with white corolla. H 4″

> *A. saximontana.* From the western United States; blue and white blossoms above glaucous foliage. H 6″

ARABIS (rock cress) — Cushion- or mat-forming plants mostly from Europe and the Middle East and blooming in early spring.

Arabis androsacea. White flowers above furry cushions of rosettes. H 1–2″

A. x kellereri. Similar to *androsacea* but cushion is grayer.

ARMERIA (thrift) — Dense mounds of stiff evergreen leaves; flowers appear for several weeks in late spring and summer.

Armeria juniperifolia (or *caespitosa*), juniper thrift. Clumps 2″ high bearing pink, white or lilac flowers. H 4–6″

ASTER — The alpine species bloom mostly in the summer.

Aster alpinus, alpine aster. From the European Alps; blue to violet flowers with yellow centers. H 6–9″

CAMPANULA (bellflower) — A large genus native to the Northern Hemisphere and blooming from June onwards. Benefits from protection against hot midday sun.

Campanula aucheri. From Asia Minor; blue-to-violet blossoms over a compact tuft of rosettes. H 3″

C. garganica. From the eastern Mediterranean; starlike blue (or sometimes white) flowers over ivylike leaves. H 4″

C. portenschlagiana, Dalmatian bellflower. Abundant 1″ light violet flowers above a compact tuft of shiny green leaves. H 4–6″

DIANTHUS (pink) — A vast genus mostly from the European Alps and flowering in late spring or early summer.

Dianthus alpinus. Large rose-pink, or sometimes white or salmon-pink, blossoms over a tuffet of shiny leaves. Prefers limey soil. H 2″

D. arenarius. Pure white fringed flowers over tight mat of grasslike foliage. H 3″

D. microlepis. Pink stemless flowers on a gray-green tuft. H 1″

DRABA — Tight, cushion-forming plants from mountains of the Northern Hemisphere and blooming in early spring.

Draba dedeana. White flowers over cushion of hairy-leaved rosettes. H 1″

D. rigida, rigid draba. Deep golden-yellow blooms over a grasslike, bristly tuft. H 2″

DRYAS (dryad) — Very small, dwarf evergreen shrubs from the Scottish Highlands, blossoming in the spring.

Dryas octopetala, mountain avens. White saucer-shaped flowers over scalloped foliage; seed heads in fall are silvery and fluffy. H 3–4″

EDRAIANTHUS (grassy bell, wheel bell) — Low-growing perennials from the Balkans that are related to the campanulas. Flowers appear in early summer.

Edraianthus graminifolius. Clusters of lavender, blue-purple or white flowers over procumbent foliage. H 4–6″

ERIGERON (fleabane) — From the mountains of North America and Europe; asterlike plants blooming mainly in the summer.

Erigeron aureus. Creeping, clump-forming plants putting out ¾-inch yellow-orange flowers. Must have acid soil. H 2″

E. compositus. White, pale blue or pink flowers over mounds of gray-green or silvery foliage. H 3–4″

E. leiomerus. Violet flowers in May, over grayish foliage. H 4″

GENTIANA (gentian) — From Europe and North America, plants noted for their deep blue blossoms mostly in spring or summer.

Gentiana acaulis, stemless gentian, spring gentian. Dark blue trumpets over shiny, broad evergreen (and mat-forming) foliage, in spring. Prefers humusy soil and protection from very hot midday sun. H 2″

GLOBULARIA — From the European Alps and the Mediterranean area, shrubby, mat-forming plants blooming in the spring.

Globularia cordifolia. Small, fluffy blue flowers in clusters above dark green mats. H 3–4″

LEWISIA — From the American West (but grow well in the Northeast), plants characterized by rosettes of thin, succulent, tonguelike leaves; most are evergreen and bloom from late spring through the summer.

Lewisia cotyledon, Siskiyou lewisia. White, pink or yellow flowers over evergreen foliage; many cultivars available. H 6–10″

L. nevadensis. White flowers rising from 2″ cylindrical leaves that are deciduous. H 3–4″

LINUM (flax) — From the Mediterranean area, summer bloom.

Linum alpinum. Chicory-blue flowers on arching stems with small gray-green leaves. H 2–6″

PENSTEMON (beardtongue) — From the western United States, a varied genus that presents foxglovelike flowers of many colors predominantly in the summer. Many species and cultivars available and appropriate, some mat-forming, others shrubby or herbaceous.

POTENTILLA (cinquefoil) — An extremely varied genus found all over the world, most bearing fingerlike leaflets in groups of five as well as five-petaled roselike flowers.

> *Potentilla alba.* Large white blossoms on 6″ stems in the summer. The matlike foliage is 5–8″ high.

> *P. fruticosa,* shrubby cinquefoil. A shrub too large for most rock gardens, but its dwarf cultivars are eminently suitable and are available in many colors. Most bloom in late spring or early summer.

PRIMULA (primrose) — A familiar large genus that includes a few alpine species. Spring bloom.

> *Primula auricula,* auricula primrose. Fragrant clear yellow flowers in May above rosettes of gray-green leaves. Prefers light shade and a continuous supply of moisture through the summer. H 4–8″

> *P. marginata.* Pale lavender or lilac flowers over a woody-stemmed plant bearing white-margined leaves. H 3–4″

PULSATILLA (pasqueflower) — From the European Alps, British Isles and North America, related to the anemones and, like them, blooming in the early spring.

> *Pulsatilla alpina.* Bright white flowers up to 2″ in diameter above a basal clump. H 8–10″

> *P. halleri.* Deep purple flowers over silky foliage. H 6–12″

> *P. vulgaris.* Large purple blossoms above a basal rosette (but cultivars are available in other colors). H 7–8″

SALIX (willow) — From Europe and North America, a large genus ranging from trees to ground covers.

> *Salix reticulata.* Tiny shrublets flower in the spring, with small, fuzzy catkins above matlike foliage. Somewhat difficult, should have steady supply of moisture. H 5–6″

SAXIFRAGA (saxifrage) — A worldwide, very large genus including many species of easy cultivation, and blooming in spring or summer.

SILENE — From the mountains of Europe, summer-blooming.

> *Silene acaulis,* moss campion. Bright pink, notch-petaled flowers from June to August above mossy cushions of foliage. H 1–2″

VALERIANA (valerian) — From Europe and elsewhere, fragrant plants that bloom in the summer.

> *Valeriana supina.* Pale pink flowers over a dense clump of oval, hairy-edged leaves. Needs steady moisture especially during the summer. H 6″

10

Small Vegetables

To anyone accustomed to the notion that a vegetable garden must be a fairly large affair, its rows stretching fifteen or twenty feet at a minimum and taking up most of the backyard, the concept of crops pushing up from a small container or appearing to burst the bonds of a tiny patch of ground only a few feet square is almost unsettling. Yet growing vegetables in cramped spaces is not only possible but highly rewarding. One can grow tomatoes in tubs at the edge of a patio, strawberries in empty milk cartons on a windowsill, lettuce in a modest window box, watermelons along a strip beside a driveway or beans on a trellis on a small apartment balcony. A copious year-long harvest of several kinds of vegetables can be gained from a single area no wider than a card table. To achieve this kind of bounty in lap-sized spaces it is necessary merely to provide the right growing conditions and to purchase seed varieties that are appropriate for small-scale circumstances. Luckily a number of seed companies have responded to the newly recognized demand for miniature or compact plants, and more new strains are being offered to the public every year, often grouped together under such headings as "space savers," "space misers" or "midgets."

Producing vegetables on a reduced scale, however, is basically a different proposition from the kind of gardening discussed in other parts of this book. Small gardens devoted to woody ornamentals like dwarf conifers, rhododendrons or heathers or to miniature bulbs or alpines are arranged and managed largely for appearance: they exist to be decorative, to please the eye. Vegetables are most often grown to reward not the eye but the palate

— or the pocketbook — and the object of the game is usually bigger (and more succulent) yields rather than handsome plants. So while corn stalks and bean bushes can make the mouth water they rarely make the eye pop, and they are not likely to be found gracing a well-designed border, although creative horticulturists have combined a few of the handsomest vegetables with flowering plants to good effect.

The greatest difficulties are practical ones. Although the leafy greens, like lettuce, can do fairly well on only four hours of direct sunlight a day, any vegetable that produces a fruit (tomatoes, beans, corn and so on) must have a solid eight hours of warming sun or its yields will be disappointing or virtually nonexistent; but that bright light does not benefit dwarf azaleas. Similarly, a friable soil mix, amply fertilized, is desirable in vegetable growing but too heady for many dwarf plants that are expected to stay small. The major problem, however, is presented by the need to turn over the vegetable garden's soil every year, in effect reconstituting it; such heavy tilling cannot be done in a bed of rock garden plants and perennials. In most cases, then, a vegetable patch must be sited differently and separated from the conventional small-scale garden.

This said, there is no doubting the fact that the smaller vegetables are worth trying, especially if space for the larger kind is at a premium. It is important to choose, however, the kind of smallness desired — whether it is the fruit or produce itself that will be miniature, or the plant that yields it.

Miniature vegetables as such are amusing and eye-catching, a novelty that many restaurants and imaginative cooks offer with great success. Some miniatures, for example cherry tomatoes, are accepted for their own sake, while a number of vegetables are of course just naturally small — radishes, for example. It is the four-inch ears of corn and three-inch carrots that truly startle the restaurant customers or the guests at a formal dinner, and indeed many of these vegetables are very tasty. But bear in mind that twice as many four-inch ears of corn are needed to satisfy a hungry eater as eight-inch ones; novelty is not very stomach-filling.

For this reason the seed companies that offer small-scale vegetables generally believe that small or compact plants that bear fruit of conventional (or modest, but not minute) size are more practical and therefore ultimately more appealing than ones that grow mere nibbles. The W. Atlee Burpee Company, for example, has concentrated on developing vining vegetables — squash, cucumbers, melons — with shorter internodes between the fruiting stems so that more fruit will grow in a given space. The Park Seed Company, a pioneer in introducing compact varieties, does no hybridizing of its own but is constantly on the lookout for reduced-size plants to offer. "We keep in touch with growers everywhere, even abroad, who are experimenting," says a Park staffer, "and if we see a good new small plant that

"Tiny Tim" tomato plant, from Burpee, is a 15-inch bush that puts out a profusion of ¾-inch fruits. (Photo courtesy of W. Atlee Burpee Co.)

produces acceptably, we'll try it, and maybe later on put it in the catalogue." While some of the smaller plants produce miniature fruit — 'Golden Midget' corn yields four-inch ears on a plant just thirty inches high — others provide full-size vegetables. 'Kentucky Wonder' bean bushes, only twelve to fifteen inches high, grow pods seven or eight inches long. Park's 'Musketeer' cantaloupe bears fruit five to six inches in diameter, but the plant is only a couple of feet across.

Because many of these plants, while smaller than normal, are not exactly midgets, integrating a vegetable-growing program with an ornamental garden will come down to a question of scale — for even a row of thirty-inch corn stalks might seem incongruous near a bed of alpine plants devised to evoke a remote mountain slope. A clear separation between the two will often be desirable, though any number of combinations are possible.

Whatever the location, there are at least four different ways to grow vegetables on a small scale. The simplest way is merely to plant small vegetable varieties in a normal garden area whose soil has been suitably enriched. Perhaps twice as many plants can be packed into an area this way as could grow in a conventional garden, with yields increasing apace. To take extra advantage of the space, grow plants vertically wherever possible: use pole beans instead of the bush variety, grow squash or tomatoes on trellises and buy the climbing varieties of peas and other vegetables. Any such garden can also include a few exotic plants like Park's 'Pepper Thai Hot' from Thailand, mound-shaped affairs eight inches high sporting bright red and green one-inch peppers that are guaranteed to take the roof off any mouth.

Another method is to tuck a few vegetables into a bed that is planted mainly to annuals — for example marigolds, which are appropriately sun-loving and also are thought by some gardeners to help control certain blights like nematodes. Shallow-rooted vegetables such as lettuce can be planted in a bed of tulips or daffodils after the bulbs have finished blooming, as their roots will cause no disturbance. At the end of the growing season the vegetable plants can be discarded along with the annuals and the upper layer of topsoil can be turned over without disturbing the bulbs.

Many small-scale gardeners, especially those who live in city apartments with limited access to outdoor space, raise vegetables entirely in containers. Aside from making gardening practical where it might not otherwise be possible at all, containers offer two decided advantages. One is the ease with which a proper soil mix can be readied using store-bought potting preparations, as each plant or minicrop will have its own individual formula. The other is flexibility of location: unless the container is quite large and heavy it can be moved around to catch the best light, either daily or as the seasons change.

The choice of container is a matter entirely of convenience and taste. All sorts of impromptu affairs can be tried, from coffee cans (with holes punched in the bottom for drainage) to bushel baskets to nail barrels, but where appearance is a factor most gardeners are likely to stick with traditional clay pots — or perhaps plastic ones — or wooden tubs if a larger planting is envisioned (and if the balcony or other supporting structure can carry them). (Do not use treated wood, however.) The size of the container can usually be computed on the basis of the plant's likely root system and the number of plants to be combined, although there will inevitably be a certain amount of trial and error involved. Ten-inch clay pots, for example, are ideal for most tomato plants.

The most promising route for many prospective growers, however — at least if they have some backyard space in which to experiment — is probably the raised bed, which combines a highly fertile growing medium with ease of maintenance. Raised-bed gardening derives from experiments made almost a century ago in France in which plants were grown in heaped-up beds composed largely of manure; the plants reacted with great vigor and produced extravagantly, and the system became known as the French intensive method.

Since then there have been many variations and refinements of the technique, but basically a raised bed is a boxed-in (or walled-in, or just heaped-up) mound composed primarily of organic substances like compost and well-rotted manure mixed with sand and conventional garden soil and further enriched by bonemeal, wood ash, fish emulsion and the like — truly a heady concoction. (A good final ratio is one-third compost or manure, one-third sand and one-third other ingredients.) Because the completed bed is elevated at least a foot above the ground level, it can be easily prepared and maintained: mixing the ingredients with a shovel is no problem and any further cultivation (which nevertheless is rarely needed) can be done by hand. If the bed is no wider than four feet (a popular dimension is four by four) all work can be done from alongside, and the soil, not being trod on, is never compacted and drains with dispatch.

The ultimate payoff, however — particularly for the small-scale gardener — comes with the yield, which is bountiful to say the least. Seeds are sown not in rows but in blocks or patches, so that plants are only two or three inches apart (their leaves provide a good mulch, obviating most weeding), and even when conventional vegetables are grown it is possible to end up with as many carrots, say, in a one-square-foot patch as would otherwise take up a twelve-foot row. When more compact varieties are grown the increase may be still more stunning.

Once you have decided what system you will adopt, you can start thinking about which crops to try. This will depend not only on your personal fancies but on how much space you can provide and how much light is available. By consulting yield charts in standard reference books you may be able to estimate what you can expect to harvest, but especially in an intensively planted raised bed all guesses will be provisional. In the main, the best advice is to start with a small planting of perhaps three or four varieties and then build from there next year.

If you are using conventional varieties to start with, it may be possible to purchase seedlings in the springtime from a garden center and transplant them directly into the garden, as with common annuals. In the case of the more specialized compact or miniature sorts, however, and with unusual vegetables of all kinds, the answer is seeds. Again the more recondite varieties will generally not be found in garden centers, and so recourse should be made to those great yearly extravaganzas, the seed catalogues. (For a partial listing of companies offering compact varieties, see the Appendix.)

In some cases seeds for the smaller plants will be grouped together for ready identifying, and some companies denote them with special markings. But often it is necessary to spot them by means of certain telltale words: instead of the pervasive "gigantic," "mammoth" and "jumbo" that fill most catalogues the trick is to search out the "midget" and the "mini," the Tiny Tims and Tom Thumbs. Entries are likely to change from year to year, but a sampling of half a dozen catalogues may turn up such delectable offerings as five-inch broccoli on plants just eight inches high (Park); cauliflower one to three inches in diameter on plants spaced less than a foot apart (Thompson and Morgan); six- to eight-inch cucumbers on mounded plants less than a foot high (Park); one-inch to one-and-one-half-inch tomatoes (bigger than the cherry type) borne on plants that can be grown in a four-inch pot (Thompson and Morgan); midget cabbage with four-inch heads (Shumway); stringless snap peas on compact bushes twenty-four to thirty inches tall (Burpee); eight- to nine-inch ears of corn on plants only three to four feet tall (Gurney's); bush-type butternut squash on vines only three or four feet long (Burpee); Tom Thumb midget lettuce with heads the size of tennis balls (DeGiorgi); or hanging basket tomato plants bred to trail attractively (Burgess).

There are admittedly some gaps. Except for carrots, none of the root crops (such as potatoes) have lent themselves to being scaled down, and a few others like celery remain similarly irreducible. But as it is there is plenty to get started with.

To get the most out of any vegetable garden — and small-scale affairs are no exception — it makes sense to draw up a planting program based on the growing spans and temperature preferences of the various crops you might raise, keeping in mind the limits of your own frost-to-frost growing season. Some vegetables (beets, early cabbage, spinach, lettuce, peas, radishes) can be planted in early spring or around the time of the last frost (seed packages will specify the preferred date) and are known as cool-season crops. But most of these suffer when exposed to warm temperatures and die off in the summer. Beans, carrots, peppers, corn, tomatoes and watermelons among others are warm-season vegetables and go into the ground after the last frost, remaining there for the balance of the growing year. Later on, many of the cool crops and a few others can be planted in midsummer to last until mid-autumn (for example beets, beans, broccoli, cauliflower, lettuce, radishes and spinach). Resourceful gardeners practice succession planting, for example growing lettuce first in a given row or section, then following it with beans or tomatoes for the warm season, and so on. But some vegetables, for example squash and cucumbers, can stay in the ground for most of the growing season.

One way to coax more output is to lengthen the growing season by starting some seeds indoors in flats on the windowsill, so that by the time the temperature outdoors has risen, the plants will have a head start. This is especially recommended in the case of tomatoes, which can be started indoors five or six weeks before the last frost.

Another trick to increase yield in a given space is known as interplanting. Two crops, like radishes and beets, are planted together in the same row or area; the radishes come up first but are harvested by the time the beets take over. And to avoid having all the vegetables of one type appearing simultaneously it is a good idea to stagger planting times, sowing only a portion of the seeds at first and others a week or two hence.

If you have opted for raised-bed gardening, the chances are that the soil will need no further conditioning or nutrients. In any other kind of bed, however, or in the case of containers or tubs, it will be necessary to turn over or till the soil thoroughly and add fertilizers before planting. After you have decided what vegetables to grow, a call to the county extension agent can tell you what kind of fertilizers will be needed as well as how often and when to apply them.

Any highly fertile bed will, of course, produce weeds in addition to the desired crops. They can be pulled by hand, but an easier way to squelch them as well as to protect plants against harmful swings in temperature is to apply a mulch. A raised bed, as previously noted, provides its own mulch by enabling the plants to be grown so close together that their foliage blankets the ground. Other beds will need an ample covering of spoiled hay, pine needles, fir bark or some other standard mulching substance. Ordinarily a mulch will be removed at the end of the growing season, but some vegetable devotees keep it in place year round and are able thereby to skip the annual laying-on each spring — as well as the yearly tilling. When planting time arrives, they merely roll back the mulch, pop the seeds in, then pull the blanket back over.

Another bane is pests and diseases, which can strike even the tiniest vegetable patch. The subject is complex and the remedies can be elaborate — indeed, many books have expounded on the theme. For the beginning grower perhaps the best course is to give the county agent yet another call, describe what you are growing and what problems you may have encountered, and follow the advice to the letter. Diligent management should preclude any large infestations, and a few bugs here and there will not do much harm.

After what should be a satisfactory year of miniharvests, it will be necessary in most gardens the following spring to till the soil all over again, or to remix the soil in any containers. The new crops should not go into the same spot as in the past year, for even in a small-scale garden crop rotation is essential — where beans grew the first year, plant broccoli, carrots or whatever. The renewed spate of work should come as no hardship, for the first year's vegetables will probably be delicious. Those who have partaken agree that while smaller may be less impressive, it can often be tastier.

11

Dwarf Fruit Trees

THE IDEA OF A DWARF FRUIT TREE in the garden — especially in a garden made up primarily of other small-scale plants — is almost irresistible. The little trees, four to six feet high, present a pleasing appearance at all times of the year, particularly in winter when their branches stand out gracefully against the bleak landscape; if they have been espaliered or trained in one of the other special forms often used for fruit trees, they are especially decorative. In the springtime they are garlanded with the unlikeliest profusion of delicate pink or white blossoms, whose fragrance can be nothing short of seductive. And to top it all off there is that wonderful annual payoff of fruit — the same size as a normal tree produces, and surprisingly copious. Few gardeners should be able to resist such a handsome and delightful plant, whose output makes such good eating.

There is a catch, however. Dwarf fruit trees are, to put it mildly, labor-intensive. If not given constant care and attention they may fail to fruit, succumb to disease or at the very least take on a distinctly scraggly look. "Oh yes," goes the oft-heard refrain, "I had a couple of them once, but I never got much fruit, and after a while they just expired." Owners must be prepared to prune them carefully at regular intervals and to spray them more often than any other garden plants. In addition, dwarf fruit trees are extremely choosy about where they can be planted. They demand full sun for most of the day (if not sun-drenched they will not bear), and they tolerate no competition; no other plants may be placed within their dripline, as they require all the nourishment their soil can give them. They tend to be frail, and may snap off at their grafting point unless firmly staked; they may

Full-size nectarines hang from a dwarf tree that has been potted for decorative effect. The tree is a Miniature Stark® Honeyglo™ (Anderhone cv.). (Photo courtesy of Stark Bro's Nurseries & Orchards Co.)

also be short-lived — dwarf peach trees simply do not last longer than eight or ten years. Any thoughts, in other words, of casually inserting a dwarf apple tree into an existing, amply planted garden area and then leaving it to its own devices should be dismissed. Under such circumstances the tree will most assuredly bring nothing but disappointment.

Yet for those willing to supply the necessary assiduous care the rewards appear to be worth it, for great numbers of dwarf fruit trees are sold every year. Commercial fruit growers in particular have taken to them, as the trees are far simpler to prune, spray and pick than their full-sized cousins, and the yield per acre can be greater — four dwarf trees can flourish in the space taken by one standard-sized one, sometimes presenting a greater total bearing surface. A well-tended dwarf apple tree, for example, may be expected to produce two or more bushels of apples a year. The dwarfs also come into fruiting at an earlier age, bearing after just a year or two of growth instead of five to eight years. So it is no surprise that Stark Bro's Nurseries and Orchards, one of the largest fruit tree growers in the United States, sells almost twice as many dwarf apple trees as full-sized ones.

At the same time, amateur gardeners willing to rise to the necessary challenges have been happy to plant dwarfs merely as ornamentals, not complaining if the fruit may turn out to be less than plentiful or even nonexistent. Any fruit at all is viewed as a plus. "And don't forget," remarked one nurseryman, "you are not going to be as demanding as the commercial grower who has to satisfy the supermarket chains. If your peaches turn out to be pitted because of some minor ailment, you won't object — they'll still taste great to you."

Urban gardeners and others with extremely cramped growing areas have found a further inducement in the form of containers. Dwarf fruit trees make fine container plants, doing well in tubs or even large pots — whose constricted space can help keep them dwarfed. Tubs do away with the problem of competition and can be placed to take maximum advantage of the sun. And in such surroundings the need for intensive care can seem far less burdensome. A city terrace may well be one of the likeliest spots for a dwarf fruit tree.

To a greater extent, perhaps, than with any other category of small-scale plants, the story of dwarf fruit trees must be told in terms of rootstocks. Except for citrus trees, which in any event are in a class by themselves, virtually all fruit trees are propagated by grafting. They do not come true from seed — plant an apple seed and what comes up will not be worth keeping — nor do they come true from cuttings. It is the rootstock that determines the eventual size of the rest of the tree — what is known in the grafting business as the scion — as well as a few other characteristics like disease resistance and hardiness.

The most successful dwarfing rootstocks are those for the apple and the pear, the so-called pome fruits, and so these are among the most popular dwarfs. Less successful are those for the stone fruits, the peach, cherry, apricot, nectarine and plum, for their rootstocks often fail to achieve much dwarfing effect or are lacking in some other way (peach trees however may be genetically dwarfed, maintaining their small stature without a special rootstock). Citrus plants — oranges, lemons, limes, grapefruit, kumquats and others — can successfully be raised from seed, but they too are often propagated by grafting as it may be more convenient for the grower.

The cultivation of dwarf deciduous fruit trees long antedates the discovery of rootstocks, however. In the third century B.C. the Greek historian Theophrastus noted the low-growing traits of some apple trees brought back from Asia Minor by soldiers of Alexander the Great, and in a later era Roman farmers widely planted such dwarfs. Natural (or genetic) dwarf fruit trees were also greatly admired in ancient China for their ornamental qualities, along with the small-scale conifers like the pines and junipers. During the Renaissance in Europe it was discovered that certain rootstocks could control the dwarfing effect, and two apple stocks became especially popular. One was the "Paradise" apple from Persia, its name most probably derived from the Persian word *pairidaeza,* meaning a park or garden. The other was the "Doucin" from the French *douce,* or sweet. So multiplied, dwarf fruits became the rage of fashion and were prominently featured in the famous gardens designed for Louis XIV at Versailles. In the nineteenth century another dwarfing stock, Jaune de Metz, was introduced in France and became widely used by fruit growers.

The trouble was that the system was unreliable: rootstocks were being crossbred and mismatched and so were becoming undependable. To clear things up, scientists at an English fruit experimentation station in East Malling, Kent, undertook in the early decades of this century to standardize all known apple rootstocks. Out of their efforts came the famous EM (for East Malling) rootstocks, designated by Roman numerals according to their characteristics and propagated by rooting shoots from a single mother plant to produce what are known as clonal rootstocks, whose performance is completely dependable. Some EM stocks were adaptations of the old Paradise and Doucin stocks, while the most dwarfing of all was EM IX, derived from Jaune de Metz. Many dwarf apple trees sold today contain the EM IX rootstock or derivations from it. Subsequently another series of rootstocks, bred principally for their disease resistance by the East Malling technicians and others in Merton, England, became the Malling-Merton stocks, known by the initials MM.

Meanwhile a parallel effort focused on rootstocks for the pear. Although it was known that a surprising number of plants to which the pear is related

— among them the hawthorn and even the cotoneaster — could be used for rootstocks with some dwarfing effect, the best was the pear's closer relative, the quince. Pear seedlings have been grafted on quinces at least since the seventeenth century in France. At the same time that the East Malling scientists systematized the apple rootstocks they also produced a quince series, designated as Quince EM followed by a capital letter. In France today 90 percent of all pears are grown on quince roots, most of them from the EM series, and a similar percentage holds true for the United States.

While they do exert a decided dwarfing effect, rootstocks like the EM series have one great drawback: their root spread is small and thus inadequate to hold the tree securely, necessitating staking or some other kind of support. So it is that fruit trees sometimes are "double-worked," or grafted in two places. In such instances, the rootstock will be that of a normal, amply-rooted tree; to it will be grafted a short segment of a dwarfing stock — known as an interstem — and then on top of that will be added the scion, or fruiting upper story. (Nevertheless, staking is still advised.) Some growers have added further refinements. Stark Bro's Nursery in effect triple-works its dwarf apples, adding a second interstem for hardiness before the scion. Thus the dwarf fruit tree that you buy at your nursery is probably two or even three or four trees joined together.

Oddly enough — considering the immense amount of effort that has gone into perfecting their performance — just why or how dwarfing rootstocks work is not really known. One theory long held is that their shallow root system partially starves the rest of the tree, taking up too few nutrients. Another is that the passages that transfer nutrients upward — call them the plant's piping arrangements — are such that the nutrients arrive in reduced quantities or in the wrong proportions. Other studies point to some kind of hormonal imbalance in the rootstock. Recent investigations have led pomologists to suspect that the rootstocks may harbor some kind of virus, probably latent, that makes them act the way they do. The searches continue.

If a contest were held to decide which kind of dwarf tree might be the likeliest for the backyard gardener to try, there would probably be a close race between the apple and the peach, with the pear coming in soon after. Partly because of the wide variety of effective rootstocks available and partly because their fruit can be put to so many uses, dwarf apples have long been best sellers; but they require constant pruning and spraying. Peaches, whether on their own roots or grafted, are much easier to care for. Pears are of course beguiling, and like apples they are prime candidates for training in unusual forms like espalier (see pages 152–153). But their quince rootstocks exert a much diminished dwarfing effect: the dwarf pear will still be about two-thirds the size of the normal tree. They are furthermore subject to winter kill and other problems.

Espalier: The Two-Dimensional Tree

One of the most intriguing aspects of fruit tree growing, and one that certainly applies to dwarf fruits, is the opportunity to train the plant as an espalier or some similar special form. The resulting trees are exquisite as they present their fruits on graceful branches trained in artful patterns against a wall. But the technique of espalier — the word derives from the Italian *spalliera,* for a support for the shoulder or back — was originally devised for practical as well as ornamental reasons. Fruit trees need sun and air to fruit successfully, and training a tree in a two-dimensional plane that faces south presents every bearing surface to the light for maximum productivity. Although the technique is frequently thought of solely in terms of trees trained in the classic manner against brick or stone walls, a fruit tree can be grown on any support from a wire fence to a wooden trellis. Fruits have been so grown commercially in Europe for centuries, generally supported on wires or wooden frames, and a surprising percentage of commercial fruit growing in the United States is also based on such practices. Many of the trees so trained are dwarfs.

While there is no limit to the possible intricate forms to which a tree can be espaliered, the most commonly used fall into two categories:

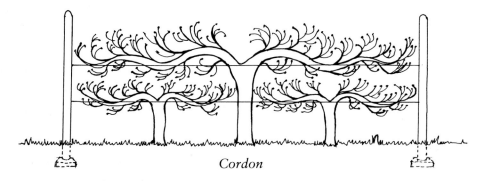

Cordon

1. **Cordons.** These are single stems (the word is French for "string") trained to grow horizontally, vertically or on a diagonal, with no side branches other than short spurs or stubs. The result is like a garland, a long

stem that will bear flowers and fruit from one end to the other. A cordon can make an elegant lining to a garden walkway.

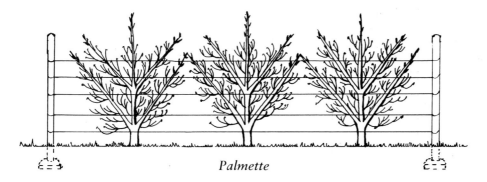

Palmette

2. **Palmettes.** These are branched trees whose limbs have been trained to spread out fanlike, more or less in the shape of a palm leaf. The traditional goblet-shaped espalier growing against a wall is technically a palmette. But palmettes may be given all sorts of decorative forms; one popular technique is to train the branches to make interconnected arches.

There are nurseries that specialize in training trees into espalier forms, but it is not difficult to produce one yourself — if you have the patience. Buy a young (perhaps one-year-old) dwarf tree — apples, pears and peaches make equally good espaliers. Plant it beneath whatever framework (south-facing, of course) you want it to grow against, whether a wall with supports attached to it, a trellis or an arrangement of wires. As the tree grows, rub off side buds as needed so as to limit growth to the stem, or train the branches to follow whatever pattern you have chosen, tying them to the frame as you go. If you are creating a palmette, prune or pinch off new growth as needed to make sure one side does not develop faster than the other. Be careful to let no unwanted side shoots get too large or they will spoil the effect. Prune the tree for maximum fruiting just like any other (see text). Espaliers are not created overnight, but in a few years you will have a creation that is all your own — not nature's — design.

Rootstocks for the other deciduous fruits — the cherry, apricot, nectarine and plum — produce an even lesser degree of dwarfing and may be subject to other ills like incompatibility: the graft eventually stops working and the tree dies. If the lure of possessing a dwarf apricot, plum or whatever proves overwhelming, a solution suggested by more than one expert is to purchase one and keep it in a container, for example a two-foot-square tub, thus limiting its growth by cramping its root system.

An important consideration to bear in mind when pondering any fruit tree purchase is that of pollination. For fruit to develop from a flower, the blossom has to be pollinated. But pollination requirements differ, some species being self-fruitful — a single tree pollinating itself — while others are self-unfruitful and require another tree nearby for fertilization to take place. Most peaches, nectarines and apricots are self-fruitful, as are some cherries: a single peach tree, for example, will produce fruit unaided. But most apples and pears and some cherries are self-unfruitful, and the second tree must furthermore be of a different variety. If you own a dwarf Delicious apple tree, in other words, to get fruit you must have a second tree that is not a Delicious. One consolation: if a neighbor owns that second variety, that's good enough. Bees travel.

Another factor is soil. Apples will do well in virtually any garden soil, but other trees are more demanding. Peaches and some plums require a light, well-drained soil; cherries can take heavier soil but it must also be well-drained. Pears and the rest of the plums, on the other hand, actually prefer a heavier soil, as does the quince rootstock. But the soil should be deep and, though well drained, capable of retaining some moisture. Fruit trees cannot stand "wet feet," but they also must not be allowed to dry out.

Because different varieties of dwarf fruits may perform differently, and because the type of rootstock can be so vital, it is especially important to buy from a knowledgeable nursery or mail-order source. The large mail-order firms specializing in fruit trees — Stark Bro's and Bountiful Ridge come to mind — have long years of experience and can be relied on, but it may be more convenient to shop locally. In that case, check your local county extension agent for names of recommended dealers. It is essential that the dealer be familiar with dwarf fruits as there are so many varieties available and some may be more appropriate for your needs than others. "A good rule," says one authority, "is to ask the dealer what rootstock was used on a tree. If he or she does not know, that's not the dealer for you."

One argument for shopping locally is your climate. Most deciduous fruits will do well anywhere within Zones 5 to 7, but in warmer areas they may perform poorly or be out of the question. In recent years, however, fruit varieties from such semitropical spots as Israel and the Bahamas have been made available and are worth investigating. Gardeners in Zones 9 and 10 should of course consider citrus plants, none of which are hardy in temperate zones.

A final thing to think about before buying, particularly in the case of apple trees, is the use to which the fruit will be put, as some varieties are better for eating while others excel for cooking or canning. A good dealer can make pertinent recommendations. Sometimes, to be sure, several needs can be met on a single tree: growers sometimes graft several varieties on one rootstock. Such prodigies are called "three on one" or "four on one" trees.

Although the big catalogue houses provide detailed instructions on planting and a good local dealer will give appropriate advice, a few guidelines are worth noting. Fruit trees are often sold bare-rooted, but that does not mean they may be stored indefinitely after purchase. If they cannot be put into the ground immediately, be sure to wet the roots — and keep them moist. So also must the root ball of a balled-and-burlapped tree be kept moist. When planting, be sure the graft union ends up above the soil line lest the scion put out roots of its own and negate the whole dwarfing effect. Mix no fertilizer with the soil at planting time: the sudden application of salts might injure the roots fatally. And unless they are to be espaliered or otherwise given special training, almost all dwarf deciduous fruit trees must be supported firmly — many commercial growers use metal pipes as stakes, to be on the safe side. (Make sure the wire holding the tree to the stake is covered with rubber hosing to prevent chafing.) If the tree is sold growing in a container, it may already be staked.

When and if you transfer the tree from one container to another or to garden soil, be sure to "distress" the roots, loosening them from the root ball, so that they will reach out into their new environment. Containers should, incidentally, be no larger than is absolutely necessary — dwarf fruits are better off if kept slightly pot-bound. One expert has observed that a twelve-inch pot is probably big enough for the first three or four years; small peach trees have fruited successfully in eight- or nine-inch containers. But bear in mind that plants in small pots are vulnerable to freezing and will probably have to be taken indoors during the cold months — or taken out of the pot, plunged into the open ground, and mulched.

It will almost certainly be advisable, if the roots have been cut in any way during planting, to cut back the top a bit at the same time. In any event, a deliberate pruning program should start at once. Deciduous fruit trees require judicious pruning to *(a)* keep them open to sunlight and air and maximize the effect of spraying, *(b)* do away with narrow-angled crotches that might cause branches to break under the weight of fruit, and *(c)* encourage the development of wood ideal for fruiting. Trees that are espaliered are so trained to ensure these qualities, but others must be pruned regularly — late winter is the best time, just before they emerge from dormancy — to keep them in prime decorative and fruiting shape. Dwarf citrus trees fortunately need little pruning beyond periodic removal of dead or diseased branches.

Both dwarf apple trees and dwarf pears should be "headed" low — their lowest branches should emerge only about a foot (at the most two feet) from the ground. So right at planting time, if such so-called scaffold branches do not exist, it is important to cut the top back to encourage them to emerge. Thereafter, similar scaffold branches should be induced to grow, coming out at wide angles if possible at intervals going up the trunk, so as to impart a kind of wineglass shape to the tree. Peaches, nectarines, plums and some cherries should be initially headed at eighteen to twenty-four inches and similarly trained at later stages. At each periodic pruning, cut away any dead or seemingly surplus wood to keep the center of the tree open to light and air, and remove any "water sprouts," shoots growing vertically from midway out on the branches, or "suckers," similar unwanted growths spurting up from the roots. Make all cuts neatly, leaving no stubs.

Peaches and nectarines require special additional attention at their annual pruning in order to keep producing the best fruit. Unlike apples and pears, which grow their fruit at the end of short spurs that emerge from the branches, peaches and nectarines do so on what is called one-year wood, new growth that has been added the previous year. It is advisable to keep such new growth coming along by cutting back existing branches regularly — not every branch, as that would cause the tree to fruit too exuberantly for its own good, but about half of them each year.

To provide protection for the dwarf tree's shallow root system as well as to discourage competitive growth, a good mulch should be kept in place at all times. Many substances will serve; one of the best is spoiled hay from nearby farmlands, if you can get it. A problem with mulches, on the other hand, is that they attract mice, who like to gnaw at the tree trunk — as do rabbits. To guard against such marauders, keep the mulch a few inches away from the trunk, and also protect the trunk with hardware cloth or an equivalent barrier.

Dwarf fruits do not demand much fertilizing, but to ensure continued health and good fruiting it is a good idea to apply a well-balanced fertilizer annually, distributing it around the dripline where the feeder roots are located. The one absolutely essential maintenance requirement is regular spraying against pests and diseases. Needs and potential ailments differ among the many kinds of trees, as do local conditions. The best bet is to ask your county extension agent for a recommended comprehensive program, and then to follow the instructions faithfully. But do not be surprised if the program calls for thorough spraying or dusting every two or three weeks throughout the growing season.

One of the anomalies of fruit production is that deciduous trees may produce too abundantly for their own good. Not only may the individual fruits thereupon turn out to be puny but there may be so many of them that they will break their branch. Dwarfs are especially given to such excess, and their fruit must be thinned methodically: it is estimated, for example, that only 10 percent of the flowers of dwarf apples and pears are needed for a full crop; with other fruits the figure is 20 to 30 percent. Thinning makes for superior fruit. One way to do it is to wait until the fruit is big enough to be inspected critically — but the sooner the better — and remove all unsatisfactory specimens (undersized, wormy or diseased); then finally reduce the overall number. On apples, pears, peaches and nectarines fruits should occur only at six- to eight-inch intervals; on dwarf plums the interval is three to four inches. Cherries, however, usually need no thinning. It is a good idea to pick apples and pears without removing the stem from the branch — this will protect the spurs. Other fruits may be removed simply by twisting them away.

As to when you may best pick the remaining fruits without running the risk of letting them drop, the usual custom is to wait until the flesh begins to appear softer and the fruit seems to be juicier. (Pears are the exception and should be picked when immature.) With apples the right time is just as a yellowish tinge begins to appear amid the red or green; with pears it is just as the dark green of the skin begins to fade to a yellowish green. The perfect moment is one that experience alone will begin to dictate. When it occurs, there is only one thing to do. Enjoy.

Some Popular Fruit Tree Varieties

(The varieties listed below are only a sampling of what might be available — and recommended — in any given temperate region of the United States. County extension agents will have more specific recommendations.)

APPLE

Summer ripening: Redfree, Prima, Lodi, Vista Bella, Jerseymac, Tydeman's Red, Akane, Summer Treat, Paulared, Gala, Royal Gala, Mollie's Delicious, Ozark Gold, Jonamac

Fall ripening: Britemac, McIntosh cultivars, Spartan, Macoun, Empire, Red Delicious cultivars, Rome Beauty cultivars, Stayman cultivars, Idared, Jerseyred, Golden Delicious cultivars, Winter Banana cultivars, Hawaii Gold, Granny Smith

PEACH

July ripening: Harbinger, Candor, Earliglo, Garnet Beauty, Surecrop, Harbelle, Jerseydawn, Redhaven, Harken, Harbrite

August ripening: Norman, Washington, Loring, Blake, Cresthaven, Jerseyqueen

September ripening: Rio-Oso-Gem, Autumnglo

NECTARINE

July ripening: Earliblaze, Summer Beaut, Harko

August ripening: Hardired, Sunglo, Redchief, Flavortop, Fantasia, Redgold

September ripening: Late Gold

PEAR

Bartlett, Bosc, Seckel, Anjou

SWEET CHERRY

Hedelfingen, Ulster, Van, Venus, Stella, Angela, Vogue

SOUR CHERRY

Montmorency, Meteor

12

Planning and Designing

ALTHOUGH SMALL-SCALE GARDENS are surely simpler to maintain than conventional ones, they are just as challenging to arrange felicitously. The placement of plants, the positioning and flow of textures, shapes and colors, the relationship of one plant to another and the appropriateness of the planting area to its surroundings — all these can be matters of concern. It might even be said, in fact, that they are of greater concern in a smaller space where every square inch counts, for the prospective viewer is inevitably closer to the plants and thus more aware of every detail.

Good design of course means different things to different people, and there are no absolutes. Stock plans that show where to place each species in an idealized border are of little use except as food for thought, for everyone's garden area is unique — and sometimes the plants recommended in

OPPOSITE: Landscape designer Bill Brady picks a bouquet of marsh marigolds at the crest of a garden he created in Sherborn, Massachusetts. It is a felicitous arrangement of plants and assorted rocks that complement each other without competing. The stepping-stone path is lined with mosses painstakingly collected in New England and with *Maianthemum canadense,* whose green shoots jut up from the moss mounds. The pines in center and center left are *Pinus densiflora* 'Umbraculifera', the Tanyosha pine. The three darker evergreens at center and center left are dwarf Norway spruces, *Picea abies* 'Clanbrassiliana', while in the right foreground is a bird's nest spruce, *Picea abies* 'Nidiformis'. The purple-flowering rhododendrons at lower left are 'Purple Gem'. (Photo by Gary Mottau)

such proposals are not readily available anyway. Furthermore, there is nothing wrong with having no declared design at all. Said one devotee whose plantings were a hodgepodge but a source of great enjoyment to him, "It's my garden and you don't have to like it."

Because most gardeners set out plants with an eye to their decorative value, however, certain design considerations are worth knowing about. Some of them are particularly relevant to dwarf plants and small gardens. For although every garden is different, the effects that plants and gardens have on the average viewer are usually predictable. So when pondering how to start a new small-scale garden, what new plants or trees to buy or where to put a plant just acquired, you may find a few guidelines to be helpful.

A key preliminary question is what purpose the proposed garden area is to fulfill. Will it be just for experiment, a place to try out new species or cultivars? Or is it for food production, a place to grow apples (from dwarf trees) or corn (from dwarf corn plants)? Or, more likely, is it intended mainly to give visual pleasure? If its purpose is decorative, from what angle will it be viewed — from the house or apartment, from a terrace or from another spot on the property? Should its emphasis be on the year-round effect of evergreens, or on flowers in season — or a combination of both?

In choosing small plants, a critical concern is their rate of growth. Some plants marketed as "dwarfs" are actually small for only a limited time; unless they are herbaceous, such products should probably be avoided. At any rate, be sure (if you can) that the dwarf characteristic is genuine. But almost any miniature or dwarf, if it is a permanent plant like a tree or shrub, is likely sooner or later to outgrow a confined space. The question is how soon it will do so.

Reputable nurseries will usually state the height that a tree or shrub is expected to reach after ten or twelve years, and the listings in this book have been devised with those figures in mind. Many dwarf conifers can be relied on to grow no higher than eighteen inches, say, in a dozen years, but some will exceed three feet or more in that time. Note also that some dwarfs, while not gaining height, will spread with considerable vigor. "It's an unfortunate fact," says Long Island nurseryman Jim Cross, "that a lot of people buy so-called dwarf weeping hemlocks expecting them to stay small, and then find that in eight or ten years the tree has covered their entire garden." But the right kind of weeping hemlock will not grow so fast, either vertically or horizontally. Paying attention to growth rates can help you to make sure that your carefully devised plan will remain pleasing for more than just a few years.

Another important consideration is soil type and treatment. In the world of dwarfs and miniatures the gardener encounters at least three different soil preferences, depending on the kind of plant being grown, and it is generally injurious to mix or combine them. Conifers, rhododendrons, heathers and other permanent plants are likely to prefer a decidedly acid soil that is humusy but is not disturbed from one year to the next. Herbaceous plants — perennials, annuals, and most ferns — thrive under such conditions too. But vegetables require a periodic turning of the soil and so must be separated from the shrubs and perennials (and from bulbs as well). Alpine plants need a fast-draining, gritty soil that is unacceptable to the others as it will never provide enough nourishment for them. In short, there is no all-purpose small-scale garden soil: cucumbers, daffodils and alpines cannot coexist in proximity (unless grown in containers). The solution is to create a garden that is specialized as to soil type; or to implant barriers in the soil to prevent mixing (a tedious task); or to make two or three separate small gardens. Far from being an irksome limitation, however, this requirement, by narrowing the choices, simplifies the otherwise formidable task of deciding what to grow.

Scale is another factor worth thinking about. Dwarf plants can seem ridiculous growing next to their much larger counterparts, and a miniature garden with its huddle of tiny plants can appear orphaned when plunked down, unaccompanied by any large rocks or other features to anchor it, in a large open area like a lawn. Plants look better when they relate sensibly to their neighbors in size and are not drowned in space. Ideally the small-scale garden should stand alone but not be forlornly isolated — admittedly a tricky matter. Good scale is often assured if the plants are set against an attractive neutral background like an evergreen hedge or an ivy-covered wall, enabling the plants to establish their own visual environment. By the same token, make sure the plants relate to each other pleasingly in their form or shape and demonstrate a good sense of proportion.

In a newly established garden there is seldom any crowding, as most gardeners are likely to buy only a few plants to start with. Later on, however, as enthusiasm builds, even a not-so-small plot can begin to seem quite cluttered. Aside from esthetic considerations, remember that plants need good air circulation. So beware of overplanting.

One way to grow more plants in a given space, however, is to reach up. The ivied wall behind the garden can be adorned with plant containers. Trellises and pergolas similarly extend the garden upward, as do hanging baskets. Climbing plants that are not dwarfs — such as clematis or climbing roses — may be useful as companions in such situations.

Planting also need not be confined to conventional garden locations. Do not ignore such unlikely spots as narrow strips along driveways, shady places under trees (a number of small perennials will thrive there), and ends of steps along a pathway, even a few square feet behind the garage. Small plants can be shoehorned into almost any constricted space.

The use of a hot color such as pink or magenta in the foreground,
enhancing the sense of depth by making other colors seem to recede,
highlights a California rock garden. The pink flowering plant is
Saponaria ocymoides, the Alpine soapwort. (Photo by Pamela Harper)

A few design precepts are worth bearing in mind. If the garden is near the house it may look better if its style relates to that structure — a formal arrangement may seem more appropriate beside a classic or very modern building, an informal one next to a less austere dwelling. To keep a garden area from appearing lopsided there should be what is known as balance: a strong feature like a specimen tree on one side can be balanced perhaps by a group of smaller trees or shrubs on the other. The two sides should probably not be identical (for pure symmetry is not always to be desired), but their visual impact should be comparable. Give a thought to the texture of the plants — the shape and look of the leaves, the density of the foliage — as this is especially noticeable in small plants. Too many plants of the same texture can be needlessly monotonous; skilled garden designers generally like to vary the textures.

While the object of a design sometimes is to make a garden seem small and cozy, often the intent is to make the limited space appear larger or at least more welcoming. To this end a number of tricks can be brought into play. A narrow space can be made more attractive and also seemingly larger by being divided into a number of sections; division into different levels has a comparable effect. Any small space will look larger if it is organized on a diagonal axis from one corner to another. A sense of greater depth can be introduced into any garden area by planting trees or shrubs with large leaves in the foreground, then trees or shrubs with leaves of decreasing size behind them; paths that grow narrower as they recede, or that are made of ever-smaller stones or slabs as they lead away, will produce the same impression.

Depth can also be accentuated through the use of colors. Hot colors, like red and magenta, have the quality of approaching the viewer, while cooler ones like blue seem to recede. Thus a border with red plants in the front and blue in back will seem to have greater depth than one with the reverse arrangement.

The actual choice of plants can often be simplified if the garden is based on a particular theme, or controlling idea. One notion is to use the planting area to evoke a much larger scene; it is a technique long since mastered by the Japanese, who can summon up windswept mountaintops, lordly forests or quiet glades in a span of just a few feet. Another route makes use of what is called plant association: in any particular environment certain plants are generally found in association with one another, and a garden limited to such plants can be highly attractive. Thus a small shady garden can be based on a selection of dwarf woodland plants like *Primula acaulis* (English primrose) or a dwarf hosta, together with some of the dwarf woodland ferns. A garden made up mainly of heaths and heathers will represent the windswept world of moors and other desolate locales, while one that features dwarf rhododendrons and such conifers as *Pinus mugo* (mountain pine) or *Abies balsamea* (balsam fir) will recall the slopes of high mountains. A rock garden given over largely to alpine plants will of course convey the mood of an upland meadow or scree. There are many other possibilities.

It may seem unnecessary to pass along the hoary admonition to draw up a rough plan of the garden before making any purchases, but the rule is well worth emphasizing. For one thing, it will make the overall choice of plants easier. For another, it will lead to a sensible purchase schedule as well as an orderly planting program.

In most gardens, small or large, that make use of several different kinds of plants it makes sense to proceed in a series of stages. The first stage is the setting out of the biggest plants, the evergreens and larger deciduous shrubs or trees that will constitute the "bare bones" of the garden. Not only does the entire design or scheme revolve around them; they also are the plants that delineate the garden throughout the year, remaining to be enjoyed through midwinter snows and bleakness after the lesser plants have disappeared or been covered up.

In most small gardens, of course, dwarf conifers are hard to beat for establishing the basic structure. They come in a multitude of shapes, from thin and upright (known as "fastigiate" in the trade) to conical, to round, to weeping (or pendulous), to spreading (or prostrate) and even to trailing or cascading — a truly amazing range that is a tremendous design asset. Their textures vary from bristly to lacy and they come in all shades of green, or even blue or sometimes yellow. Most are admirably slow-growing and can be depended on to remain in scale for many years.

Their very slowness of growth can admittedly be a problem, as a conifer counted on to become a mainstay of the garden may remain a pipsqueak for too long a time. Jim Cross has a suggestion. "If you are starting a garden," he says, "you may want to save up and buy an older dwarf conifer or two to begin with — they will cost a bit more, but you'll have a better-looking garden at the outset."

Along with the large evergreens you will probably also want to position any rocks that are essential features of the design. How you do so is purely up to you, and there are no set rules except that it is usually a good idea to have the grain of any series of rocks running in the same direction. But good rock placement can make all the difference. Remarked a renowned British landscape expert to a nursery owner whom he was visiting, "I will give you top marks for your nursery and the up-to-date propagating department, but your so-called rockery is but a heap of stones." One way to find out how rocks can be attractively set into a garden — as well as to pick up random design tips on how to set plants out — is to visit botanical gardens, good specialty nurseries or well-known private gardens and see how the experts do it.

After you have positioned the major plants (and rocks) that form the basic structure, the second stage is taken up with filling in the intervening spaces with any smaller evergreen or deciduous trees, shrubs or plants that will round out the general design. This is the time to install any backdrop or protective windscreen and to plant smaller evergreens like heathers and any ground covers that may seem appropriate. Bear in mind that the silhouette formed by the garden's permanent plants at the back of the garden will be particularly noticeable in winter, and that many shrubs look better when planted in groups of two, three or four than singly. As for ground covers, it is worth mentioning that although most do not qualify as miniatures or dwarfs in the strictest sense — they just happen to be low growers — several are good companions for small-scale plants. Among them are *Ajuga reptans* (carpet bugle), *Vinca minor* (periwinkle, or myrtle) and the smaller forms of *Euonymus fortunei.*

The final stage comes with the setting out of herbaceous plants, whose role for the most part will be to provide seasonal decoration and color. But this group may also include some herbs, which are not discussed in this book; a few low-growing ones like *Origanum majorana* (oregano, or sweet marjoram), *Mentha spicata* (spearmint), or *Thymus vulgaris* (thyme) may fit conveniently. It also of course includes any bulb plants, which for the most part can be set in any spot where their usually brief burst of color will be welcomed.

As to the choice of colors and their orchestration through the seasons, there can be no strict guidelines, for everyone's taste is special. It might be well to mention, however, that the blooming times of flowering shrubs and heathers should be taken into account in any succession of bloom. And many experts suggest that a beginning gardener might want to limit his or her flowering plants to those that are in the same general color range, like various shades of blue and purple (white is a safe accompaniment, too), and introduce contrasting colors with caution.

A few special situations should be mentioned. Heathers are spreading plants and should be set out according to the advice given in chapter 5, allowing enough space between plants to prevent overcrowding — they will cover the ground soon enough. Heather enthusiasts have suggested that as the native heaths where these plants originate are likely to undulate in attractive ways, you may want to mound up the soil gently here and there and set the plants in such a way as to provide a naturalistic feeling. If they are planted on a slope and several varieties are used, little else need be done to make the display a pleasing one, as the different textures and hues can provide a show in themselves.

Entrance doorways can be effectively embellished by plantings of dwarf conifers, whose usefulness is enhanced by their slow growth rate. A pair of

Potted plants and various dwarf and low-growing species handsomely adorn a modern poolside setting in Massachusetts. (Photo by Gary Mottau)

OPPOSITE: Rocks placed judiciously grace a New England garden of small plants. (Photo by Gary Mottau)

fastigiate (slim and erect) yews or junipers, for example, may seem ideal flanking the door. But make doubly sure you have varieties whose growth rate is predictable, lest the trees begin expanding laterally and make passage inconvenient.

The same caution should be exercised if you are contemplating foundation plantings. Most contemporary dwellings have very low or unobtrusive foundation stonework instead of the traditional kind that cried out for a heavy screen of shrubs or trees — which often grew up to block the view from indoors — and so dwarf conifers have seemed an ideal planting for the modern building foundation. Again, however, check the trees' growth rate, and consider using some of the weeping or spreading varieties in addition to

those of conventional conifer form. If the roof of the house overhangs the planting area the soil there will tend to be dry; in such cases the low-growing junipers are useful as they require less moisture than other species.

Note also that dwarf rhododendrons, azaleas and such other small ornamentals as dwarf laurel, box, pieris and broom (see chapter 4) make excellent additions to any foundation planting, not to mention miniature roses (chapter 6) and the many small herbaceous plants (chapter 8). On the other hand an array of tiny plants marching along in front of a sizable house can threaten to become monotonous, and you may want to plant one or two slightly larger specimens, perhaps at the corners away from the windows, or a deciduous tree (like a dwarf Japanese maple) set several feet from the wall to provide not only some needed height but depth as well.

As a final touch to any small-scale garden, be aware of the decorative value of certain mulches. Although many different kinds of substances can be used as mulches, from leaf mold all the way to black plastic, a regard for overall appearance may point to some of the handsomer materials like cocoa bean hulls or fir bark (or, in the case of any alpine garden, pebbles or aggregate). Using the same mulch throughout will also help lend a feeling of unity to the entire display.

13

Boxes and Troughs

FOR EVERY GARDENER who has the luxury of actual garden soil for
growing small-scale plants, there is at least one who cannot spare the
extra space, or whose soil is unsuitable and uncorrectable, or who
inhabits an apartment with no yard of any kind but with a balcony, terrace
or similar outdoor area. For any such person, or for someone who would
like a different kind of small garden where certain special plants can be
separated from the rest, the answer of course is containers. But instead of
setting dwarf plants out singly, one to a container (which would sometimes
have to be minuscule), many enthusiasts like to combine them into miniature collections — dish gardens, lilliputian rockeries, diminutive mountain
scenes, even pygmy rose gardens — which not only are extra-small but are
usually movable. Best of all for some gardeners, these arrangements can
be installed on a raised surface for easy maintenance and close-in viewing.

Three kinds of extra-small gardens are worth special attention. One might
be called the pot garden: an assemblage of small plants growing together in
any modest container. A second is that old standby, the window box, in this
case given over largely to dwarfs and miniatures. The third, and perhaps the
most attractive, especially for devotees of alpine plants, is the trough garden.
It consists of a planter box that any do-it-yourselfer can make using a very
light concrete mix, and with proper protection it will keep its plants healthy
right through the coldest winters.

There is no limit, of course, to the kinds of containers that can be used
for pot gardens: washtubs, wheelbarrows, cookie tins and plastic cartons
are just some of the objects that have been pressed into service. What will

be appropriate is a matter of taste, but a few realities can affect one's choice. Because such containers will often be set out on pavements or decks in full sunlight, metal should be avoided as its tendency to heat up can injure root systems, especially those of small plants. Both unglazed clay and wood escape this flaw; clay has the added advantage of "breathing," so that oxygen and moisture both reach the roots more efficiently. Any wood surface that will come in contact with soil must be treated with a preservative to prevent decay; but do not use creosote as it is toxic to plants, and do not use treated wood of any kind for growing vegetables for the table.

The size of the container governs its ability to withstand temperature extremes, particularly cold. Plant roots are nowhere near as hardy as their tops, and so root protection is the key to bringing most plants through the winter outdoors. In any region where the temperature may fall below 10 degrees Fahrenheit it is a good idea to allow a minimum of fourteen inches of container soil in any direction, horizontally or vertically, regardless of the size of the plant. If still lower temperatures are to be expected, even larger

OPPOSITE: A border of dwarf plants is accompanied by three troughs bearing even smaller plants. (Photo by Gary Mottau)

The yellow blossoms of golden fleabane, *Erigeron aureus,* are surrounded by sedums, sempervivums and (at top) a dwarf conifer, plus rocks and a piece of driftwood, in an artfully planted trough garden. (Photo by Pamela Harper)

containers must be provided, or insulation installed — or the plant must be hauled indoors during cold spells.

Because plants grown in containers do not have the benefit of nutrients that will be available in the soil of a larger garden area, their soil must be richer than that normally provided for garden plants. A good formula is two parts garden loam or potting soil to one part peat moss (or leaf mold) and one part sand (or perlite or vermiculite), with a touch of bonemeal added. Good drainage is a must, and you may want to install a layer of aggregate or pebbles in the bottom of the container before adding the soil mix; if the drain hole is inadequate the pebble layer should be several inches thick. But container soil tends to dry out rapidly in the open air. City gardeners in particular will want to pay special attention to watering in the summer — in hot spells it may have to be done daily — and to washing the leaves every week or so to remove soot and other pollutants.

Somewhat similar strictures apply to window boxes. Many city dwellers have no other opportunity to garden outdoors, but they can maintain flourishing minigardens outside their windows using either conventional annuals or some of the dwarf varieties described in this book. Wood is by far the best material. (Garden centers sell plastic boxes but they are often too narrow to provide adequate root room and protection against the heat of the summer sun; metal again is out.) A good window box should be at least eight inches wide to allow for more than one row of plants, but anything wider than about ten inches may be too heavy, especially if the box is to be hung on brackets. Boxes should be at least seven or eight inches deep to provide for root development and effective drainage. Three or four feet is a reasonable length: a longer box will be too heavy to lift out when the soil is to be replenished, although you can trowel out the soil in such cases, leaving the box in place.

Apartment dwellers should find out whether their landlord permits window boxes; some cities also place restrictions on all outdoor planters, for example forbidding the placing of containers on fire escapes. Make sure all brackets are securely anchored to the building structure and that the box in any event cannot be dislodged from its perch accidentally. Note also where any runoff water will fall and be sure it does not cause problems with neighbors or pedestrians beneath.

Although most garden centers sell workable wooden boxes, many people like to make their own — for one thing it assures achieving a design that will go with the house. Boxes are ideally constructed of cedar or redwood, which are resistant to rot, but both are expensive; clear pine or fir is acceptable if it is treated with a preservative, and so is marine plywood (which is waterproofed). Use one-inch stock — it is actually three-quarters of an inch thick — and brace it with one-inch strips at the inside corners, or with angle irons. Drill half-inch drainage holes about every six inches in a zigzag row along the bottom, and if the box is to sit on a ledge or sill nail wooden strips to the bottom to level it or raise it for drainage. You may want to glue the pieces together with a good waterproof glue before securing them with brass screws; the glue will help prevent water from seeping out through the joints.

Some box owners, to forestall runoff problems, devise trays that fit under the boxes to catch the drainage water and that are removed for emptying. Another scheme is to install a makeshift gutter under the drainage holes to carry the water off to the side, where it can be collected in a basin or can drain away harmlessly.

The finished box can be either stained or painted, but light colors are preferable to dark as they reflect light and make for cooler conditions in hot weather. As with other containers, a layer of pebbles or pot shards over the drain holes is to be recommended, and the soil should be equally rich, with bonemeal or a well-balanced fertilizer added.

Because the box will inevitably be too shallow to protect plants through subfreezing winter temperatures, the plants to be grown are normally limited to annuals and such perennials as you do not mind discarding at the end of the year. (The soil in any event should be thoroughly cultivated and replenished each spring.) There are, however, at least two ways to circumvent this limitation. One is to take cuttings in the fall, pot them and hold them indoors until springtime. The other requires access to a conventional garden area and involves the use of metal planting trays that will fit into the box. They can be made of galvanized iron and should be at least six inches deep; metal is permissible in this instance as the wooden box provides adequate insulation. Miniature roses, perennials and even spring-flowering bulbs can be planted in such trays and plunged into the garden when not needed, or for overwintering. When the appropriate moment arrives the tray can be retrieved and placed in the window box to provide a seasonal show; after the blooms have gone the container can be returned to the garden, to be superseded by another in the box.

Such cold-weather problems are avoided by trough gardens, which are large enough and well enough insulated to protect most hardy plants against freezing. The idea originated in England, where gardeners years ago found that old stone sinks and abandoned stone watering troughs made highly attractive planter boxes. Alpine plants looked especially good in them as the stone evoked the upland terrain. For a while, as horses gave way to autos and old-fashioned kitchen sinks were replaced by modern fixtures, genuine troughs were easy to find, but the bona fide article is rare today or prohibitively expensive. Handsome equivalents can nevertheless be made of a special lightweight mix, which is called hypertufa as it resembles porous tufa rock — though it is much easier to manipulate.

A fully planted trough garden two or three feet long will admittedly be heavy, weighing more than a hundred pounds, but it can still be moved as whim, changing design requirements or seasonal availability of light may demand. The result is the smallest, and some gardeners would say the most beguiling, all-weather garden possible. Many possessors of conventional gardens keep a trough or two for displaying certain special plants, as troughs can be given over to dwarf woodland plants, bog plants or even desert plants aside from their customary assortment of alpines. Almost any miniature plants except for spreaders and those with wide-ranging root systems are worth trying in them. For city dwellers or anyone with a terrace or deck, they are a boon.

Some garden centers and specialty nurseries sell ready-made hypertufa troughs (either fully planted or empty), but it is easy to make one at home. All you will need is two wooden frames like shallow boxes (they should preferably be bottomless, but in any event, one should be a couple of inches smaller all around than the other), some one-inch or two-inch wire mesh, a couple of dozen long wood screws, half a dozen short (three or four inches) half-inch dowels and the materials required for the mix — cement, peat moss and perlite or vermiculite.

It is a good idea to make the walls of the trough about two inches thick and six to eight inches high on the outside. The larger wooden frame should have inside dimensions equal to the trough's outside measurements, and should be screwed together from its outside; the other should have outside measurements equal to the trough's interior dimensions and should be screwed together from its inside (corner posts or angle irons will be needed for this). The wire mesh, which will be used for reinforcing, should be made into a rectangular basket whose measurements are two inches less than the trough's overall dimensions; secure its corners with extra wire. (Thus for a trough 2 feet long, 18 inches wide and 6 inches high, the larger frame should be 24 by 18 by 6 on its inside, the smaller 20 by 14 by 4 on its outside, and the wire mesh 22 by 16 by 4.)

Place a large sheet of plastic on a firm level surface (like a basement floor) and set the larger frame on it. Mix the hypertufa ingredients using one part cement to one part vermiculite to two parts peat moss; don't worry if what you mix does not suffice, as more can be prepared when needed. Add water slowly until the mix is pliable but not runny. Cover the plastic within the frame with enough mix to make a layer one inch deep, then set the wire

OPPOSITE: A robust small juniper, *Juniperus communis* 'Compressa,' rises out of a trough that also contains the flowering *Erinus alpinus* and, sprawling over the near edge, *Cotoneaster mirophyllus*. (Photo by Pamela Harper)

mesh basket on top of the mix, making sure it is equidistant from the frame all around. Push the dowels down through the mesh and the mix wherever you will want drain holes. Add another one-inch layer of mix from wall to wall, then set the inner frame on top of it, making sure it too is equidistant from the outer frame. Fill the wall cavity with mix all the way to the top, poking it down with an old knife or stick so that it goes into all the corners and embeds the wire mesh completely. Smooth the top, cover the entire affair with a sheet of plastic or a tarpaulin, and let it sit until the mix is semi-set, which is usually eighteen to twenty-four hours.

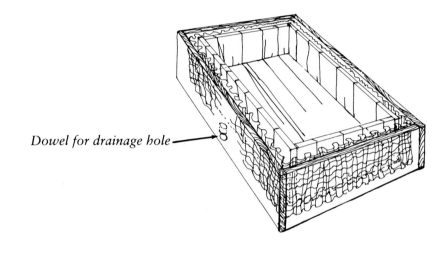

Dowel for drainage hole ———

To make a trough, construct two boxes, one smaller than the other, plus a wire basket that will fit in the space between them. The hypertufa goes into the intervening space, with the wire reinforcing it. Make drainage holes by setting dowels into bottom; they can be knocked out when the mix has dried.

After this period, remove the inner frame by unscrewing the sides from each other and gently knocking them away from the hypertufa. Remove the drainage plugs by twisting and lifting them, and cover the trough again for another twenty-four hours.

Now you can unscrew the outer frame sections and knock them away. Using a stiff wire brush, roughen the sides and top to give them texture. Then cover the trough again and leave it for at least three days — until the hypertufa is completely hard. When it is, tip the trough up on its end, clean out the drainage holes and brush the bottom edges to remove any excess material. You can also round off any other edges with a rasp. Rewrap the trough and let it stand for at least two weeks. Finally, cure the concrete (which otherwise could harm plant roots) by stoppering the drainage holes with corks and filling the trough with a mixture of water and potassium permanganate (half an ounce of permanganate crystals for every three gallons of water), letting it stand for twenty-four hours and then rinsing it with fresh water. The trough is now ready for use.

The forgoing instructions will result in a handsome planter that will offset small plants quite satisfactorily. There are other ways to make a trough, however. One with a very rough finish can be made simply by digging a hole in the ground that is the exact size of the prospective trough, fashioning a wire mesh basket whose dimensions are slightly smaller all around, lining the hole with hypertufa mix, setting the basket in place and then covering the wire mesh, all by hand, until you reach the top edge; in all other respects the procedure is the same. Virtually any size or shape of planter can be made using some variation of the procedure. But quite a different approach was devised by an elderly gardener in Pennsylvania, Charles Becker, who wanted a trough with almost featherweight lightness: he coated a styrofoam chest (the thick kind in which steaks are sent through the mails) with epoxy glue, to which he applied dry sand. The finished box, empty, weighed less than six pounds.

A technique comparable to Becker's can also be used to convert any discarded porcelain sink — a genus not noted for its beauty — into a surprisingly pleasing planter trough. All you need to do is coat the outer surfaces of the sink with a bonding agent (hardware stores can recommend a good brand), plus as much of the inner surface as will show above the soil; then while the bonding agent is still tacky, simply pat the hypertufa mix onto the coated surfaces and allow to dry. The former ugly duckling will look for all the world like a fine old stone sink.

Before adding soil, you may want to move the trough to its eventual location, as it is lighter when empty. Many gardeners set their troughs on pedestals of one sort or another, or on ledges or parapets, to bring them closer to eye level. Troughs should if at all possible be set in an open area, where they will get plenty of sunlight, and away from the dripline of trees or roof overhangs. If you are going to plant alpines or dwarf conifers, the soil mix recommended by the Oliver Nurseries (see chapter 9) is a good one; if ericaceous plants (heathers, rhododendrons and others) or woodland species will predominate, a better mix is one part granite grit, two parts gritty sand, one part peat moss, one part leaf mold or compost and one part garden soil. Otherwise the container mix set forth earlier in this chapter might be in order. A layer of small stones or pot shards should be placed immediately over the drainage holes (which should themselves be covered with screening or broken pot pieces); cover the drainage layer with burlap or similar material, then fill the trough with your soil mix. It is a good idea to mound the soil slightly on top, as it will settle a bit in time.

Arranging the plants in a trough is no different from setting them out in any other garden — the area is just much smaller. All the guidelines apply that were set forth in the previous chapter. But you may want to visit specialty nurseries or alpine collections to see how others do it. Most trough devotees like to place a rock or two somewhere in the trough, burying them somewhat for a natural look. Another popular recourse is to build the design around a dwarf conifer or two — some of the extremely small junipers or firs will do well. After that the possibilities are endless.

Assuming the trough is set out in the open, it may need little watering other than a generous soaking at the outset; but if it is subject to hot sunlight and dry winds in the summer, it may require a daily drenching. Above all, make sure it does not dry out in hot weather. Fertilizing with fish emulsion or a similar complete feeding in April and again in July should keep the soil healthy and fertile; every year in the spring add a topdressing to the soil mix. When winter comes and plants go dormant, tilt the trough slightly (you can put a small rock under one edge) to aid drainage. The hypertufa should make the trough impervious to frost, but it is a good practice to cover it with pine boughs, salt hay or some other porous material during the coldest months. When warm weather returns, pull back the covering and enjoy your coffee table–sized miniature garden.

Appendix

Some Specialty Nurseries

(▲ = No mail order.)
(Note: Most nurseries refund catalogue price with order.)

DWARF CONIFERS

Coenosium Gardens, 30590 S.E. Kelso Rd., Boring, OR 97009 (Catalogue $3)
Dilatush Nursery, 780 Route 130, Robbinsville, NJ 08691 (Phone eves. for
    appt.: (609) 585-5387) ▲
Foxborough Nursery, 3611 Miller Rd., Street, MD 21154 (Phone for appt.:
    (301) 836-7023)
Girard Nurseries, Box 428, Geneva, OH 44041
Honey Run, Layton, NJ 07851
Hortica Gardens, P.O. Box 308, Placerville, CA 95667
Michael A. & Janet L. Kristick, 155 Mockingbird Rd., Wellsville, PA 17365
    (Phone eves. for appt.: (717) 292-2962)
Oliver Nurseries, 1159 Bronson Rd., Fairfield, CT 06430 (Catalogue $1) ▲
Powell's Gardens, Route 2, Box 86, Princeton, NC 27569 (Catalogue $1.50)
Rakestraw's Gardens, 3094 S. Term St., Burton, MI 48529 (Catalogue $1)
Rice Creek Gardens, 1315 66th Ave., N.E., Minneapolis, MN 55432 (Cata-
    logue $1)
Rocknoll Nursery, 9210 U.S. 50, Hillsboro, OH 45133 (Catalogue $.44 post-
    age)
Siskiyou Rare Plant Nursery, 2825 Cummings Rd., Medford, OR 97501 (Cat-
    alogue $1.50)
Washington Evergreen Nursery, Brooks Branch Rd., Leicester, NC 28748 (Cat-
    alogue $2)

DWARF RHODODENDRONS AND AZALEAS

Baldsieffen Nursery, Box 88, Bellvale, NY 10912 (Catalogue $3)
The Bovees Nursery, 1737 S.W. Coronado, Portland, OR 97219 (Catalogue
    $2)
Carlson's Gardens, Box 305, South Salem, NY 10590 (Catalogue $2)

The Cummins Garden, 22 Robertsville Rd., Marlboro, NJ 07746 (Catalogue $1)

Greer Gardens, 1280 Goodpasture Id. Rd., Eugene, OR 97401-1794 (Catalogue $2)

Hall Rhododendrons, 1280 Quince Drive, Junction City, OR 97448 (Catalogue $1)

Holly Heath Nursery, Box 55A, Calverton, NY 11933

E. B. Nauman, 688 St. David's, Schenectady, NY 12309

Orlando Pride Nurseries, P.O. Box 1865, 145 Weckerly Rd., Butler, PA 16001 (Catalogue $1)

Westgate Gardens Nursery, 751 Westgate Drive, Eureka, CA 95501

Weston Nurseries, East Main St. (Route 135), Hopkinton, MA 01748 ▲

Whitney Gardens & Nursery, P.O. Box F, Brinnon, WA 98320-0080 (Catalogue $1)

ALSO: Girard, Oliver (see Dwarf Conifers, above)

WOODY ORNAMENTALS

Broken Arrow Nursery, 13 Broken Arrow Rd., Hamden, CT 06518

Middle Country Gardens, 130 Paul's Pass, Coram, NY 11727   ▲

ALSO: Hortica, Kristick, Orlando Pride, Powell's, Rocknoll (see Dwarf Conifers and Dwarf Rhododendrons and Azaleas, above)

HEATHS AND HEATHERS

Daystar, Litchfield-Hallowell Rd., Litchfield, ME 04350 (Catalogue $1)

Heather Acres, Inc., 62 Elma-Monte Rd., Elma, WA 98541

White Flower Farm, Litchfield, CT 06795 (Catalogue $5)

ALSO: Powell's (see Dwarf Conifers, above)

MINIATURE ROSES

Jackson & Perkins Co., 83A Rose Lane, Medford, OR 97501 (Note: sells own roses only)

Miniature Rose Co., Rose Ridge, Greenwood, SC 29647

Mini Farm, Rt. 1, Box 501H, Bon Aqua, TN 37025

MiniRoses, P.O. Box 4255, Sta. A, Dallas, TX 75208

Nor'East Miniature Roses Inc., 58 Hammond St., Rowley, MA 01969 *or:* P.O. Box 473, Ontario, CA 91762

Rosehill Farms, Galena, MD 21635

Sequoia Nursery, 2519 East Noble Ave., Visalia, CA 93277

MINIATURE BULBS

Bakker of Holland, U.S. Bulb Reservation Center, Louisiana, MO 63353

Burpee Seed Co., 231 Burpee Bldg., Warminster, PA 18991

The Daffodil Mart, Rt. 3 Box 794-R, Gloucester, VA 23061 (Catalogue $1)
DeJager Bulbs Inc., 188 Asbury St., S. Hamilton, MA 01982
John D. Lyon Inc., 143 Alewife Brook Pkwy., Cambridge, MA 02140
McClure & Zimmerman, 1422 W. Thorndale, Chicago, IL 60660
Potterton & Martin, Nettleton, Nr. Caistor, N. Lincs. LN7 GHX, England
    (Catalogue $1 in currency)
Quality Dutch Bulbs Inc., 52 Lake Drive, Hillsdale, NJ 07642
John T. Sheepers Inc., 63 Wall St., New York, NY 10005
Van Bourgondien Bros., Route 109, Babylon, NY 11702
Wayside Gardens, 503 Garden Lane, Hodges, SC 29695-0001
ALSO: Rice Creek, White Flower Farm (see Dwarf Conifers and Heaths and
    Heathers, above)

HERBACEOUS PLANTS

Kurt Bluemel Inc., 2740 Greene Lane, Baldwin, MD 21013 (Catalogue $1)
Busse Gardens, 635 E. 7th St., Cokato, MN 55321 (Catalogue $1)
Carroll Gardens, 444 E. Main St., Westminster, MD 21157 (Catalogue $2)
Garden Place, 6780 Heisley Rd., P.O. Box 388, Mentor, OH 44061-0388
Maver Rare Perennials Nursery, RR 2 Box 265B, Price Rd., Asheville, NC
    28805 (Note: seeds only. Seed list $2)
MSK Nursery, 20066 15th Ave. N.W., Seattle, WA 98177 (Phone for appt.:
    (206) 546-1281) ▲
Nabel's Nurseries, 1485 Mamaroneck Ave., White Plains, NY 10605 ▲
Andre Viette Farm & Nursery, Route 1, Box 16, Fishersville, VA 22939 (Cat-
    alogue $1.50)
ALSO: Daystar, Powell's, Rakestraw, Rice Creek, Rocknoll (see Dwarf Conifers
    and Heaths and Heathers, above)

ALPINE PLANTS

Famosi Nursery, Lowell Davis Rd., Wilsonville, CT 06255 ▲
Fjellgarden, P.O. Box 1111, Lakeside, AZ 85929 (Catalogue $1)
Owl Ridge Alpines, 5421 Whipple Lake Rd., Clarkston, MI 48016 (Catalogue
    $.50)
ALSO: Daystar, Maver, Oliver, Rakestraw, Rice Creek, Rocknoll, Siskiyou (see
    Dwarf Conifers, Heaths and Heathers, and Herbaceous Plants, above)

MINIATURE VEGETABLES

Mail-order seed companies:

Burgess Seed & Plant Co., 905 Four Seasons Rd., Bloomington, IL 6¹701
DeGiorgi Co., P.O. Box 413, Council Bluffs, IA 51501
Farmer Seed & Nursery Co., P.O. Box 129, Faribault, MI 55021
Gurney Seed & Nursery Co., Yankton, SD 57079

Harris Moran Seed Co., 3670 Buffalo Rd., Rochester, NY 14624
Nichols Garden Nursery, 1190 North Pacific Hwy., Albany, OR 97321
George W. Park Seed Co., Greenwood, SC 29647
R. H. Shumway, 628 Cedar St., Rockford, IL 61105
Thompson & Morgan, P.O. Box 1308, Jackson, NJ 08527
ALSO: Burpee (see Miniature Bulbs, above)

DWARF FRUIT TREES

Bountiful Ridge Nurseries, Princess Anne, MD 21853
Stark Bro's Nurseries and Orchards Co., Louisiana, MO 63353

Plant Societies

American Conifer Society, c/o Mrs. Maxine Schwarz, Box 22, Severna Park,
    MD 21146
North American Heather Society, c/o Alice Knight, 62 Elma-Monte Rd., Elma,
    WA 98541
American Rhododendron Society, c/o Mrs. Paula L. Cash, 14885 S.W. Sunrise
    Lane, Tigard, OR 97224
American Rock Garden Society, c/o Buffy Parker, 15 Fairmead Rd., Darien, CT
    06820
American Rose Society, Jefferson Paige Rd., Shreveport, LA 71119

For Further Reading

Atkinson, Robert E. *Dwarf Fruit Trees Indoors and Outdoors.* New York: Van
    Nostrand Reinhold Co., 1972.
Austin, Robert, and Ueda, Koichiro. *Bamboo.* New York: Walker/Weatherhill,
    1970.
Bacon, Lionel. *Alpines.* Newton Abbot, Devon: David & Charles, 1973.
Bawden, H. E. *Dwarf Shrubs: A Gardener's Guide.* Woking, Surrey: Alpine
    Garden Society, 1980.
Brookes, John, ed. *Garden Design.* New York: Simon & Schuster, 1984.
Brookes, John. *The Small Garden.* New York: Macmillan, 1978.
Brooklyn Botanic Garden, *Dwarf Conifers. Handbook on Miniature Gardens.
    Handbook on Small Gardens for Small Spaces.* Brooklyn: Brooklyn Bo-
    tanic Garden, various dates.
Cox, Peter A. *Dwarf Rhododendrons.* New York: Macmillan, 1973.

Del Tredici, Peter. *A Giant Among the Dwarfs*. Little Compton, RI: Theophrastus, 1983.

Doerflinger, Frederic. *The Bulb Book*. Newton Abbot, Devon: David & Charles, 1973.

Farrelly, David. *The Book of Bamboo*. San Francisco: Sierra Club Books, 1984.

Fitch, Charles Marsden. *The Complete Book of Miniature Roses*. New York: Hawthorn Books, 1977.

Foster, F. Gordon. *Ferns to Know and Grow*. Portland, OR: Timber Press, 1984.

Foster, H. Lincoln. *Rock Gardening*. Portland, OR: Timber Press, 1982.

Foster, Raymond. *Rock Garden and Alpine Plants*. Newton Abbot, Devon: David & Charles, 1982.

Genders, Roy. *Miniature Bulbs*. New York: St. Martin's Press, 1963.

Gentile, Arthur C. *Plant Growth*. Garden City, N.Y.: Natural History Press, 1971.

Grace, Julie, ed. *Ornamental Conifers*. Portland, OR: Timber Press, 1983.

Gray, Alec. *Miniature Daffodils*. New York: Transatlantic Arts, 1961.

Greer, Harold E. *Greer's Guidebook to Available Rhododendrons*. Eugene, OR: Offshoot Publications, 1982.

Harper, Pamela, and McGourty, Frederick. *Perennials: How to Select, Grow and Enjoy*. Tucson: HP Books, 1985.

Heath, Royton E. *Rock Plants for Small Gardens*. London: Collingridge Books, 1982.

Heriteau, Jacqueline. *Small Fruit and Vegetable Gardens*. New York: Sterling Pub. Co., 1975.

Hills, Lawrence D. *The Propagation of Alpines*. New York: Pellegrini & Cudahy, 1950.

Hornibrook, Murray. *Dwarf and Slow-Growing Conifers*. Sakonnet, RI: Theophrastus, 1973.

Hoshizaki, Barbara Joe. *Fern Growers Manual*. New York: Alfred A. Knopf, 1975.

Hume, H. Harold. *Hollies*. New York: Macmillan, 1953.

Ingwersen, Will. *Alpine and Rock Plants*. London: J. M. Dent, 1983.

Ingwersen, Will. *Ingwersen's Manual of Alpine Plants*. Eastbourne, Sussex: W. Ingwersen and Dunnsprint Ltd., 1978.

Jaynes, Richard A. *The Laurel Book*. New York: Hafner Press, 1975.

Johnson, Arthur T. *Hardy Heaths*. London: Blandford Press, 1956.

Johnson, Hugh. *The Principles of Gardening*. New York: Simon & Schuster, 1979.

Knight, Frank P. *Heaths and Heathers*. London: Royal Hort. Soc., 1972.

Lawrence, Elizabeth. *The Little Bulbs*. New York: Criterion Books, 1957.

Lee, George S. *The Daffodil Handbook*. Washington, DC: Amer. Hort. Soc., 1966.

Loewer, H. Peter. *Growing and Decorating with Grasses*. New York: Walker & Co., 1977.

Lucas, I. *Dwarf Fruit Trees for Home Gardens*. New York: A. T. DeLaMare, 1946.

Mathew, Brian. *Dwarf Bulbs*. New York: Arco, 1973.

Moore, Ralph. *All About Miniature Roses*. Kansas City, MO: Diversity Books, 1966.

Ortho Books. *All About Bulbs*, 1981. *All About Vegetables*, 1980. *Award-Winning Small-Space Gardens*, 1979. San Francisco: Ortho Books.

Ouden, P. den. *Manual of Cultivated Conifers*. Boston: Kluwer, 1982.

Pinney, Margaret. *The Miniature Rose Book for Outdoor and Indoor Culture*. Princeton: Van Nostrand, 1964.

Proudley, Brian and Valerie. *Heathers in Colour*. New York: Sterling Pub. Co., 1983.

Rix, Martyn, and Phillips, Roger. *The Bulb Book*. London: Pan Books, 1981.

Schenk, George. *The Complete Shade Gardener*. Boston: Houghton Mifflin, 1984.

Schenk, George. *Rock Gardens*. Menlo Park, CA: Lane, 1984.

Scott, George Harmon. *Bulbs: How to Select, Grow and Enjoy*. Tucson: HP Books, 1982.

Skelsey, Alice. *Cucumbers in a Flowerpot*. New York: Workman Pub., 1984.

Southwick, Lawrence. *Dwarf Fruit Trees for the Home Garden*. Charlotte, VT: Garden Way Pub., 1972.

Stone, Doris. *The Lives of Plants*. New York: Scribner, 1983.

Swartley, John C. *The Cultivated Hemlocks*. Portland, OR: Timber Press, 1984.

Taloumis, George. *Outdoor Gardening in Pots and Boxes*. Princeton: Van Nostrand, 1962.

Tampion, John. *The Gardener's Practical Botany*. New York: Drake, 1973.

Teuscher, Henry. *Window-Box Gardening*. New York: Macmillan, 1956.

Thomas, Graham Stuart. *Perennial Garden Plants*. London: J. M. Dent, 1976.

Thomas, Graham Stuart. *Plants for Ground Cover*. London: J. M. Dent, 1977.

Titchmarsh, Alan. *The Rock Gardener's Handbook*. Portland, OR: Timber Press, 1983.

Tukey, Harold B. *Dwarfed Fruit Trees*. New York: Macmillan, 1964.

Underhill, Terry L. *Heaths and Heathers*. Newton Abbot, Devon: David & Charles, 1971.

Vertrees, J. D. *Japanese Maples*. Forest Grove, OR: Timber Press, 1978.

Welch, Humphrey J. *Manual of Dwarf Conifers*. Little Compton, RI: Theophrastus, 1979.

Wyman, Donald. *Dwarf Shrubs*. New York: Macmillan, 1974.

Wyman, Donald. *Ground Cover Plants*. New York: Macmillan, 1970.

Zwinger, Ann, and Willard, Beatrice. *Land Above the Trees*. New York: Harper & Row, 1972.

Index